Pat Armes,
Wishing you abundant
of blessing and success.
Thanks for being one
of Air Atlanta's loyal
Customers

In the
ARENA

In the
ARENA

The High-Flying Life of Air Atlanta
Founder Michael Hollis

Deborah Mathis with Julius Hollis

X

Plutus Partners LP

Plutus Partners LP, P.O. Box 767040, 8920 Eves Road, Roswell, Georgia 30074

Visit our Web site at www.michaelhollisbook.com

Printed in the United States of America

First Printing: November 2016
10 9 8 7 6 5 4 3 2 1

Library of Congress Cataloging-in-Publication Data
Mathis, Deborah with Julius Hollis
 In the Arena : The High-Flying Life of Air Atlanta Founder Michael Hollis / Deborah Mathis with Julius Hollis.

Print ISBN: 978-1-48358-589-5
eBook: 978-1-48358-590-1

Cover design by Joe García
Cover Photo: The New York Times, 1985, Chuck Rogers ©

For Every Young Entrepreneur Who Dares to Reach for the Skies

FOREWORD

I remember once overhearing someone ask Michael Hollis about his political affiliation. We had just wrapped up a big event in Atlanta and had gone back to Michael's place for drinks and conversation.

"Are you Democrat, Republican or Independent?" she asked.

His answer has always stuck with me because it was so telling and so true:

"I'm a capitalist," he said.

It's not that Michael would have ever bypassed the chance to engage in politics. He would never have settled for being a mere spectator of a system that conferred and consolidated power and access – two things he understood and respected. But, no political party owned him because, as he said to my friend when they first met long ago, his real identity was as an entrepreneur who was fascinated with the business world, studied it, understood it and, yes, mastered it. That's how he could be a friend to Jimmy Carter, the Democrat, and also admire Ronald Reagan, the Republican. That's why he had a certain appreciation for Richard Nixon. It was the capitalist in him who directed his political allegiances. Who was good for business was the question, because Michael knew his numbers. He knew how to count.

If there is any one quality that I had to name in defining Michael, it would be "nerve." The man was bold and audacious and knew no fear when it came to both his entrepreneurial vision and how he carried himself. Michael Hollis broke the mold of business possibilities for African Americans and he demolished the boundaries. He was the originator of the sky's-the-limit mentality for black Americans with the entrepreneurial gene. None of us had done anything as big and bold and ambitious as Air Atlanta. Michael did not just think outside of the box, he said to hell with the box.

He may have had a brilliant mind, a degree from Dartmouth and a law degree from the University of Virginia, but it still took a lot of nerve to be a 27-year-old African-American and announce that you're going to start a commercial airline. At that time, maybe only a handful of black folks even owned an airplane; but here was a young man talking about owning an entire airline. That's nerve by any standard. Dartmouth and the University of Virginia should have classes about this young man because not only was he smart, but nothing stopped him. He was so far ahead of the game.

It definitely took nerve for Michael to walk into all of those executive offices on Wall Street and convince them to put up tens of millions of dollars for Air Atlanta. That had never been done before Michael Hollis came to town.

It was even risky for him to have such a high profile in the cut-throat world of big business. He didn't shy away from publicity and attention as some would have, considering the racial and political climate at the time.

I am overjoyed that his story is finally being told because people need to know about the things he accomplished, the airline he built, the other businesses he ran, the money he raised, the lifestyle he lived, the history he made. There's a lot of instructive material here for other business owners, for business educators, for students, for any person who has a big dream but is not sure how to make it come to pass.

If you're looking for a saint, put the book down. Saints don't waltz onto Wall Street aggressively with a little money and a giant plan to face off with the big boys. Saints aren't puffed up with so much self-assurance and guts that it leaves people speechless. Saints don't keep going when they face a setback or two. Saints haven't come out of nowhere and built a world-class airline by the time they are thirty years old. Saints don't move into two floors of the most luxurious condos in the city to show the world what brilliance looks like when it's finished. Saints lay low, take the humble road. Saints don't rock the boat. As you will see, Michael was no saint; he was a capitalist, and he was genius at it.

My only surprise is that it has taken this long to tell the whole story about a business maestro who was truly one of a kind. That's an overused term, but it is the right one for him. I am proud to have called him my friend and just wish he had lived on because there was more amazement coming; I'm sure of that.

—Clarence Avant

The "Godfather of Black Music," Film Producer, Entrepreneur

Impossible is just a big word thrown around by small men who find it easier to live in the world they've been given than to explore the power they have to change it. Impossible is not a fact. It's an opinion. Impossible is not a declaration. It's a dare. Impossible is potential. Impossible is temporary. Impossible is nothing.

– "The Greatest," Muhammed Ali

ACKNOWLEDGMENTS

Writing a book is an incredible, daunting challenge even when enthusiasm for the work is high. But some stories have to be told to set the historical record straight, to make it complete, or to authenticate it. This is one of those instances.

The authors are at a loss for words to adequately convey our gratitude to the many individuals who put their busy schedules on hold to share reminiscences, photographs, documents and observations about Michael Hollis. In particular, Michael's old friends and associates Dan Kolber, Gary Love, Kimberly and Todd Alexander, Janis Perkins, Dr. Roy Keith, Jr., Eldrin Bell, Kent Matlock, Thelma McClenton, and Vicki Palmer provided indispensable assistance in recreating Michael's amazing journey from southern obscurity to international acclaim. And not once did they balk at our repeated requests for help.

Of course, none of this would have been possible without the Hollis family and its treasure trove of documents, videos, photographs, notes and other raw material that helped animate the telling of this complex story and this complex man. Just as Julius Hollis was to Michael in so many business deals, the Hollis family was invaluable to this project—Virginia Elaine, Flem, Jr., Dorothy, and Jeanne Hollis, and Patricia Arnold, especially.

There are many more to thank as well—men and women who had heavy demands on their time already, yet who were willing to drop everything and scour their memories so they could share their recollections and thoughts about complicated business deals, fun times and, sometimes, personal and private matters with us. We especially thank Congressman Jim Clyburn, Mayor Shirley Franklin, Secretary Alphonso Jackson, George Dalley, Morris Finley, and the Hollis brothers' business godfather, Clarence Avant, for their priceless contributions to this book.

Of course, we are forever grateful to our families—spouses, children, grandchildren, siblings—for their undying support, patience and understanding during the months of intense research, interviews, travels, meetings, writing and editing. We were able to accomplish this often at the expense of normal familial obligations, but they never made us feel guilty about it, but rather, sustained us and cheered us on.

Family is everything indeed.

CHAPTER 1

Bathed in the early morning rays of a hot June day, the massive smoked glass panes diffused the light across Horizon Sanctuary as solemn music gushed from the church's magnificent pipe organ. For nearly two hours, the smartly dressed Who's Who of Atlanta strolled through, proceeding somberly down the aisle to the front of the church where Michael Robinson Hollis lay in repose.

Most of the mourners paused at the open casket for only a few seconds, sometimes mouthing an adieu, a thank you or a prayer before moving on to their seats. Construction magnate Herman J. Russell, one of Georgia's richest men and the first among peers when it came to thriving black businesses, stopped at the casket and lingered there for several minutes—speechless, motionless, as if lost in reflection. He had to have noticed that Michael looked significantly smaller than when Russell had last seen him, back before pancreatic cancer had struck and reduced a strapping, larger-than-life, energetic man to 160 pounds. Perhaps he was recalling the young Michael Hollis with whom he had launched an AM radio station back in the late1980s. Maybe he simply wanted one last, lingering look at the man who, in a town where bold commercial ventures were as common as dogwoods, had zoomed past even the high ceiling of Atlanta chutzpah to create the country's first and only commercial airline ever founded and operated by an African-American.

Ebenezer Baptist was not Michael's church. He and his siblings had been raised under the banner of the United Methodist faith as members of Warren Memorial, founded in 1874 and situated on the West side of Atlanta, a mere two city blocks from the campus of historic Morehouse College. Michael had considered himself a loyal member of Warren Memorial even though he was not much of a church-goer in his later years. But, practically and symbolically, Ebenezer seemed to be the right setting for the final homage to one of the city's favorite sons, particularly one who had embodied the savvy, confidence, resilience and clout that so often made the difference between becoming a game-changing entrepreneur and being merely a dreamer. Particularly this one, who had done something no one else had dared to try. Thirty years earlier, when he was only 27, Michael had conceived and breathed life into Air Atlanta, one of the most ambitious and intriguing business enterprises ever attempted by a person of color in the United States.

Anticipating a large turnout of relatives, friends, business associates, politicians, classmates, mentors and protégés, Michael's family knew the obsequies called for not only a substantial venue but also a significant one. As with his life, Michael would want his death to leave a lasting impression on future generations of black entrepreneurs who would need his kind of tenacity and audacity to overcome the racial barriers preventing black entrepreneurs from harvesting the financial rewards that accrue to full participants in first-tier businesses. Michael had personified Sir Sidney Poitier's admonishment, "Don't be as good as; be better than. And raise the risk level." A home-going celebration at one of the country's most famous and historic churches—honorably nicknamed "the Black Vatican"—was only fitting for someone of his caliber.

Just across the street from this modern sanctum stood the congregation's historic edifice, "Old" Ebenezer. The church had been founded in 1866, rising near Auburn Avenue on a street named Airline—a sweet irony considering the decedent's claim to fame. It was from the old church, on an April day forty-four years prior, that a worldwide television audience had witnessed hundreds of luminaries—an amalgam of actors and singers, government officials, and civil rights activists—bid farewell to the Reverend Dr. Martin Luther King, Jr., who had attended Sunday School, been baptized and was ordained at Ebenezer, joining his indomitable father as co-pastor.

In 1964, when he was just a boy, Michael had met Dr. King at Ebenezer when the Hollis family attended the wedding of Thelma Reynolds, a neighbor who had grown so close to them that they informally adopted her as a cousin. For a time in her teens, Thelma lived with the Hollises, babysat the younger children while their mother worked, and ran errands for their maternal grandmother, the formidable Henrietta Moncrief Robinson— "Dear," they called her—who also lived with them and cooked and cleaned up a storm.

In giving her hand to fellow Atlantan Charles D. McClenton, Thelma had chosen her home church, Ebenezer, as the venue for the November 14th nuptials. The Pastor's Study had been reserved for a small wedding party and the bride and groom arranged for senior pastor Reverend Martin Luther King, Sr., to officiate. Thelma and Charles grew fretful upon learning when they arrived that the pastor was not there. To their relief and amazement, they were told that Martin Jr. would take his place.

At age 35, Dr. King was already a world-renowned figure, having famously faced down frothing, punishing segregationists in Montgomery, Birmingham, Greensboro, Atlanta and Albany. (Selma was yet to come.) He had already burrowed into history with a speech for the ages at the March on Washington in 1963 – a year that began with the young civil rights leader on the cover of *Time Magazine* as its "Man of the Year." In less than a month, he would ascend a stage in Oslo, Norway to accept the Nobel Prize for Peace for his leadership in the nonviolent movement for civil rights. And here he was, performing the marriage ritual for a young woman from the West End area of Atlanta and her groom.

Eleven-year-old Michael was dumbstruck by the serendipity of meeting Dr. King in person and the excitement he felt that day would reemerge every time he told of the meeting for the rest of his life. So awed was he, that even though he was just a kid, Michael told his older brother, Julius, that his brush with Dr. King had inspired him to do something special with his life and find a way to make things better for black people as his idol and newfound friend had done. His chance meeting at the big church on Auburn Avenue had stirred something.

Auburn Avenue was, indeed, a dreams-come-true zone. Throughout the first half of the 20th Century, it was a bastion of black pride and empowerment in Atlanta – a gateway to the part of town that boasted four distinguished, pace-setting black colleges where many of black America's most celebrated achievers had been educated. Auburn was the city's hub of black commerce and culture, from African-American-owned and -operated barber shops, eateries, and mortuaries, to banks, insurance companies, and nightclubs. There, for nearly one hundred years after Reconstruction, faith, ambition, and willpower coalesced into a model of black power and accomplishment elsewhere unseen in the United States, with the possible exception of Harlem, New York, where African-American art and enterprise had exploded into an acclaimed, storied "renaissance" during the 1920s and 1930s. With much less fanfare, "Sweet Auburn" had surpassed and outlasted even Harlem in its concentration of black wealth and achievement. As the century made its turn, Auburn was still so vibrant and prosperous that, in 1956, *Fortune* magazine dubbed it "the richest Negro street in the world."

Desegregation in the 1960s and 1970s chipped away at Auburn's exclusivity, opening new frontiers of possibility and expanding the options for Atlanta's black homeowners and entrepreneurs. With that, Sweet Auburn's long run as the fulcrum of African-American achievement in Atlanta faded away.

✈ ✈ ✈

Completed in 1999, the new Ebenezer Baptist Church struck an imposing and neoteric contrast to the old, shuttered monuments to Auburn Avenue's halcyon days. Proudly displaying its modernity, the new structure featured a soaring, scalloped roof; 55-foot-high, Ethiopia-inspired bell tower; landscaped gardens; tranquil courtyards; and touches of African art—designs that curtsied to Ebenezer's traditions while also signaling that times had changed. The expansive Horizon Sanctuary whence Michael would be dispatched to heaven was at once elegant and reverent, with a seating capacity of nearly 2,500.

The absence of membership privileges at Ebenezer had been but a small hitch to Julius, who took charge of his younger brother's final arrangements. As usual with the Hollis brothers, not having ready access to people, places or things required only that they tap into their large network of friends and associates to find someone who could deliver. Accordingly, Julius called upon Thelma McClenton to make the official inquiry about hosting Michael's funeral service at her home church and to ask if the Reverend Dr. Raphael G. Warnock, Ebenezer's dynamic senior pastor, would officiate. Julius was right to assume that Thelma would not hesitate to do him this favor. Of course she would ask, she assured him, confident that the church would give its consent, as it did at once.

At precisely 10:30 a.m., Dr. Warnock and several ministers flowed down the center aisle past the pews filled with mourners, pausing briefly at the draped bier upon which rested Michael's ivory casket, its lid now closed and adorned with a cascade of red, white and green flora.

Michael's family followed the clergy and settled into six pews. Among them were Julius and his wife, Jeanne; sister Virginia Elaine ("Elaine" to her family); sister Joan Hollis Mitchell and her husband, Sylvester; half-brother Flem, Jr., and his wife, Dorothy; and a host of nieces, nephews and cousins. Although not everyone noticed, the family was keenly aware of one vacancy in its fold. By the time the family members had assembled to begin their procession into the church, all of them knew that Dena, Michael's wife, was not coming.

Julius was shocked and furious, but not surprised. As far as he was concerned, Dena had no sense of propriety nor, for that matter, of common decency. From the start, he, Jeanne, some other relatives and close friends had been leery of Dena and her worrisome hold on a man who otherwise seemed far too smart to fall for it. After all, he had been the consummate eligible bachelor—intelligent, accomplished, rich, adventurous and handsome—and he fully exploited it by often romancing women known for beauty and brains. Julius thought Michael and the petite, slender Dena Freeman made for a curious pairing. From what he could tell, Dena had little to no interest or fluency in the fine arts, politics and business landscape in Atlanta, which mattered so much to his brother. Nearly ten years younger than Michael, Dena seemed to possess only a certain mystique, if that's the right way to characterize her tendency to take off for days or weeks at a time to destinations and for purposes that were, most often, couched in secrecy.

Only once had Michael expressed any reservations about the Chicago woman he had met years before in a Piggly Wiggly grocery store in Hilton Head, South Carolina, where he kept a retreat. It happened when Michael and Dena, who had been dating for a while, attended her family reunion in Chicago and he learned from one of her uncles that Dena had been married before. It bugged Michael that she had not shared that information with him. Yet, despite his unease with his girlfriend's enigmatic past, Michael continued the relationship even as Julius wondered – sometimes aloud – what other secrets Dena might have.

Julius had learned only two and one-half months earlier that Michael's long, flourishing bachelorhood was over. He had no idea that his brother was married until March 30, 2012, the day their mother died.

Every member of the Hollis family thoroughly adored Virginia Robinson Hollis. They revered her as a resourceful, perpetually optimistic woman who taught her children to study hard, grasp opportunity, do right, stick together and worship the Lord. Even though she had lived a long and fruitful life, her death at age 87 was a blow to the children she had birthed, provided for, protected and molded as a single mother leaning on her faith, hard work, the assistance of her own devoted mother, and a community that practiced the "village" approach to raising children.

Julius was on a business trip in Dubai when Jeanne called with the sorrowful report that spring day. His mind immediately began churning through the logistics of getting back to Atlanta as quickly as possible but turned to his siblings once his flight arrangements were handled. He was especially concerned about Elaine, who had made it her mission to spend all day, every day with her mother once Mrs. Hollis moved into a nursing home following a series of debilitating strokes. The nursing staff had grown accustomed to Elaine's constant presence and the sumptuous homemade meals she brought with her each day, often making enough to share with her mother's caretakers and even occasionally with other patients. Elaine was heartbroken but okay, Jeanne said, reassuringly.

And what about Michael? By then, he was in the throes of cancer and undergoing regular treatments at Grady Memorial Hospital, the place of his birth and now, the repository of his hopes for survival. How was Michael coping? Julius asked.

As the youngest child in the family, Michael had been extraordinarily close to his mother, not only in childhood but throughout his life, as even the most unsentimental business colleague could attest. Everyone with more than a passing alliance with Michael was aware of his exceptional and generous allegiance to his mother and her sublime affection for him. Mother and son were so entwined that Elaine had long ago asked friends to be on standby for the eventual day Mrs. Hollis took her leave and the family would need all hands on deck to console Michael.

Julius was relieved to hear that Michael, too, seemed to be managing alright, though Jeanne noted that the news might not have sunk in yet.

They should keep an eye on Michael, given his own delicate condition, Jeanne and Julius agreed.

"By the way, did you know he and Dena are married?" she asked, already knowing the answer.

"What? Married? When?" Julius said, his voice dripping with incredulity.

"I'm not sure, but recently. I think in the last few weeks or so."

Julius' temples throbbed. So much shock to absorb in the course of a few minutes. His precious mother had succumbed to age and infirmity. His younger brother, under attack by a relentlessly villainous disease, had acquiesced to a woman few in the family trusted. And he was eight thousand miles away. He had to get home.

Once back in Atlanta, Julius pulled his brother aside to ask him why in the world, after years of dating and living together, he and Dena had decided to marry. "He said he *had* to marry her," Julius recalled, "or she wouldn't take care of him."

To Julius, Jeanne and others, that made no sense; in fact, they found it offensive. The family's dedication to Michael's care and healing had long been evident and was unquestionable. They had been there for him all of his life and now, when that life was on the line, they had only stepped up their attention to and caring for Michael. It was true that Dena had lately been around for Michael's day-to-day care and no one underestimated the toll that can take on even the ablest and most devoted helpmate. But, to Julius and Jeanne, Dena was hardly indispensable. And the idea that

Michael felt compelled to strike a bargain with his girlfriend—a marriage bargain, no less—in order to keep her around suggested that, unusually, the master negotiator had blinked.

Their apprehensions about the marriage turned to loathing on the day of Mrs. Hollis' funeral, when Michael's new bride was nowhere to be seen. Already wracked by grief, Julius could take no more and confronted Michael about Dena's unconscionable dereliction. Even as interment was underway, he could not contain his anger, demanding to know what possible reason Dena could have for not attending the funeral of her new husband's beloved mother.

Perturbed by the outburst and possibly grappling with his own misgivings, Michael tried to explain that Dena was not constitutionally equipped to handle bereavement and loss. Years before, he said, she had not attended her own mother's funeral.

The disclosure only made Julius seethe. Rather than calm his roiling temper, Michael's defense only inflamed it.

"She wasn't at her own mother's funeral and she won't be at yours," Julius thundered at his brother.

Now, as he sat in the front pew of Ebenezer to celebrate Michael's life, Julius fully regretted the dust-up with his late brother. Still, waves of contempt for Dena continued to billow and ebb. Even Elaine struggled to make sense of Dena's slight and she had been one of her sister-in-law's few apologists. Not that she could explain the attraction either, but having spent more time with Michael and Dena than anyone else in the family,

Elaine was convinced that the two enjoyed one another's company. She had overheard them laughing and talking many times and had witnessed their affection often enough that, whatever the depth of the couple's relationship was, she believed there was something genuine there. Now, however, even the devoutly religious, gently tempered Elaine suffered surges of disgust over Dena's no-show.

Although he remained mindful of his demeanor, his body language, his gestures, and facial expressions, and listened intently to the prominent speakers singing Michael's praises, Julius kept thinking about the theory that Dena was simply too devastated to attend the service. Julius found it ridiculous. To him, her absence was an act of abject disrespect, classless-ness, selfishness and ingratitude, a public embarrassment that could not be justified. A lot of work had gone into making the service meaningful, memorable and honorable. Scores of distinguished men and women had come to pay tribute and christen Michael's legacy. This was the final scene in his brother's incredible life story and Dena's absence threatened to mar the painstakingly laid plans.

Only when the Reverend Dr. Warnock rose to acknowledge the let-ters, resolutions, and other condolences from prominent people and nota-ble institutions across the country did Julius' anger subside. Knowing there would be questions and whispers as people realized Dena was not there, he had given the pastor a heads-up about the situation and asked him to somehow convey that Dena's distress left her unable to participate in the valediction for her husband. As repulsive as that borrowed excuse was to Julius, it was the only one he could muster.

"Pray much for Sister Dena Freeman Hollis who is emotionally devastated at this time," Reverend Warnock told the assembled mourners. "We remember her in prayer." That was all.

The awkward business now behind him, Julius focused his eighteen–minute eulogy on remembrances of his younger brother. He recalled Michael's portentous childhood with its glimpses of the bright, creative mind and self-assuredness that would be the hallmarks of Michael's adulthood.

He told the church about Michael's earliest business ventures. How, at age ten, Michael began making cakes with Dear and sold them throughout the black community with the assistance of Virginia Hollis' employer, Dr. Harvey B. Smith, Jr., a respected black dentist with a big Chevy station wagon made available for delivering the baked goods to customers just in time for Thanksgiving, Christmas or other special occasions. He talked about their mother and grandmother, the twin pillars of strength who had encouraged, cajoled, guided and prayed the Hollis children into abundance. He talked about Michael's meeting with Dr. King. "It was as if he had been to the mountaintop and personally met Moses," Julius said.

Julius spoke proudly of his brother's uncanny talent for networking and strategizing, his spot-on sense of timing and his supreme self-confidence. He explained how a black man launching an airline from the home turf of aviation giant Delta Airlines had been like "Daniel entering the lions' den." He told the congregants that his brother had remained positive and determined even as cancer stripped his body of its strength and vitality. He talked about how much the family loved him, admired him, had been blessed by him and would miss him. He did not mention Michael's missing widow.

"Well done, my brother," Julius said in closing. "I'll see you up yonder."

CHAPTER 2

How a poor black boy who used to sell clothes hangers, bundles of thread, and homemade cakes to make ends meet became an insuppressible, pioneering business virtuoso is the story of not only Michael Hollis' extraordinary brilliance, ambition, and timing, but also of Atlanta's fateful transformation from a city that reserved its best for a chosen few into a city that was left no choice but to share the wealth.

From early on, Atlanta was different from other cities of the Deep South and even the rest of Georgia for that matter, because the engine of its economy was not agriculture but rather trade and transportation. Established as "Terminus" in 1837 when it was the end of the line for the Western and Atlantic Railroad, the town in short order became the main railroad hub for the South's freight and passenger trains. Its unimaginative name didn't last long, but the city prospered. The success of the railroad brought working men and their families to town. Within two years, a general store was up and running and modest homes had appeared. Doctors and druggists moved in. Barbers and haberdashers commenced business. Taverns were set up and the city's first hotel opened its doors in 1845.

Within 20 years of its founding, the city had a bank, a newspaper, a theater and a medical college, all of which were peripheral to the main commercial enterprises—railroads, mills, and foundries. Still, the constancy and variety of new establishments helped create a culture of entrepreneurship that would come to define the city renamed Atlanta.

Indeed, its magnetism as a haven for business was so powerful that even some enslaved men and women tested the waters and they were allowed to sell goods and services in town as long as they complied with the hidebound racial caste system.

But in late 1864, when General William Tecumseh Sherman's Union troops overran the wooden fortress around Atlanta and left the city in ashes, palisades and all, the southern empire seemed lost for good. The utter destruction of their city and the Confederacy's surrender five months later left white residents and business owners stunned, homeless and destitute. They quickly set out to rebuild the city – 150 businesses were up and running within one year of the conflagration – but white Atlantans nursed a grinding resentment of the newly liberated black citizens who, as they saw it, had claimed an undeserved prize at their expense. Undeterred by the Union victory, whites were just as committed to reasserting their considerable upper hand over black people as they were to restoring their homes and businesses, freedom be damned.

Not all was under their control, however. By an act of Congress, the federal government took custody of Dixie's affairs after the war and part of its charge was to enforce the newly endowed rights and privileges of black people, who were anxiously exploring freedoms theretofore only at best imagined. Most often, the new franchises came with conditions that reaffirmed an ethos of white supremacy and entitlement. Nevertheless, blacks in Atlanta and throughout the dismantled Confederacy seized opportunities, doing their best to believe that the "New South" so zealously championed by Atlanta newspaper editor Henry Grady might actually come to pass. The Reconstruction Era brought Freedmen's Bureaus, Equal Rights Leagues, and black men to the Georgia Legislature. Newly emancipated blacks poured into the city, leaving behind plantations that had been segmented into sharecropping plots or other southern sites where hateful new "Black Codes" made it a life-and-death matter to so much as look a white man in the eye.

Atlanta, they had heard, had three private institutions of higher learning for people of color—Atlanta University, Clark, and Morehouse (Spelman and Morris Brown wouldn't open until after Reconstruction)—with some of the brightest stars of the black intelligentsia in place to train and invigorate the mind. In Atlanta, black parents might be able to send their young children to the Gate City School down on Armstrong Street while they went to work, perhaps at one of the flourishing black businesses in town. There were spots to hear music and cut a rug on Saturday night, then on Sunday mornings, the family could power up their spirits at one of the several churches founded by people who shared their experience, sang their kind of songs and preached their kind of sermons. Atlanta, they heard, was the ticket.

One such believer was Alonzo Herndon who, at age 20, left his share-cropping family in tiny Social Circle, Georgia, and headed west, eventually alighting upon Atlanta in 1883 with a pocketful of savings from barbering jobs he had held along the way. Just as he had heard, Herndon discovered that the state's bustling capital city was fertile ground for business and it seemed to welcome any legitimate and respectable new venture irrespective of who owned it, provided everyone stayed in his or her place.

Now in a city with as much opportunity as a former slave could expect from a sweetheart of the Confederacy, Herndon opened a barbershop alongside white-owned businesses downtown, albeit under protocols so absurd that he was beholden to enter his own establishment by the back door.

Reconstruction flickered out after little more than a decade, undermined by recalcitrant lawmakers in both the protected states and the nation's capital. With race relations left to their own devices, black and white Atlantans continued their day-to-day engagements amidst growing tensions as city and state officials installed new or resurrected laws that stripped away many of the African-Americans' newly acquired rights.

The pressure cooker exploded in downtown Atlanta on a late September evening in 1906 when a mob of whites began attacking African-American men, women, and children willy-nilly in a fit of violence that consumed two days. Enraged by rumors that black men were serially assaulting white women—an apocryphal tale being repeated across the South at the time—attackers beat, kicked, strangled or shot to death at least

25 black persons, by some accounts more. Among the dead was a barber who worked across the street from Alonzo Herndon's shop. As luck would have it, Herndon had closed up early that day and was at home when the furor started.

The 1906 riots left Atlanta's white establishment warier than ever about black liberation and surer than ever about segregation. It hurriedly put new restrictions in place, deepening the color line and pushing black Atlantans even farther away from of the city's core. Many black businesses left downtown and retreated to black-dominated sections of the city near the nest of black universities or to Auburn Avenue where Henry Rucker, the federal government's only black revenue collector, had already built a multistory building with space to lease and where other African-American establishments had taken root. Auburn Avenue's rapid assemblage of black enterprise in the wake of the riots set it on its legendary course.

Just seven years after the turmoil, Herndon, going against trend, re-made his place on Peachtree Street into a new palatial barbershop and spa, the likes of which had seldom been seen anywhere. The Crystal Palace with its mahogany, crystal, porcelain and leather appointments, its twenty-five custom-made chairs and twenty baths, its nickel and marble boot-black stands, its impeccably uniformed all-black barbering staff, was so glorious that not only did it attract the city's top business leaders, judges, and physicians as patrons, but it was also a magnet for tourists who had to see the extravagant salon for themselves. Herndon may have built it to strut his wealth and panache and as a thumb in the eye to the guardians of white privilege as much as to make money, but even he could bend the rules only so far. Services at the Crystal Palace were pricey, a luxury the average black man could never afford. Herndon would have to rely on white customers to keep the business running and that meant he could not serve black ones. Such was the law.

Sweet Auburn's welcome mat was well-trod in the 1920s. By then, the avenue boasted two bank buildings; doctors, dentists and lawyers' offices; a pharmacy, a mortuary, and several restaurants; the country's first black-owned daily newspaper; and Alonzo Herndon's Atlanta Life Insurance Company, a business that made him the city's first black millionaire with an exquisite, custom-built Beaux Arts mansion to show for it. His building on Auburn Avenue, along with the Rucker Building, the Citizens Trust Bank, the Odd Fellows Building, and the Prince Hall Masonic Temple, gave testament to African-Americans' determination to have what had been studiously and ferociously denied them: an opportunity to shine.

It was an ideal environment for the likes of John Wesley Dobbs—a driven, self-assured, college-educated, Savannah-born transplant who had broken into the middle class by way of his job as a railway clerk for the U.S. Postal Service. With his election as the Grand Master of the Prince Hall Masons of Georgia, Dobbs joined the exclusive cadre of influential African-Americans who had taken it upon themselves to act as agents, spokesmen, decision-makers and pacesetters for black Atlanta with Auburn Avenue as their command post. Dobbs would come to be known, affectionately and deferentially, as the "Mayor of Sweet Auburn," the leader of an elite cartel that included Alonzo Herndon's son and successor Norris Herndon; lawyer A.T. Walden; businessmen T.M. Alexander, Lorimer Milton and Clayton Yates; Auburn Avenue pastors Martin King, Sr. of Ebenezer and William Holmes Borders of Wheat Street; and William Cochrane, head of the city's only black YMCA.

All of the men were fervently devoted to black empowerment and justice and believed their privilege obliged them to use the respect and access they enjoyed at City Hall for the benefit of their beleaguered race. It would be Dobbs and his fellow godfathers in the room whenever the affable and energetic Mayor William B. Hartsfield deigned to entertain black interests.

Image and possibility were everything to William Hartsfield. Throughout his six-term mayoral reign and beyond, he was a tireless, even shameless, booster and promoter of the city, trumpeting it as not only the ultimate destination for big business but the beau ideal of American commerce itself. For Hartsfield, one guarantor of the bright future he envisioned was an airport of unparalleled size and service that would make Atlanta an indispensable crossroads. Another was to ensure that the city's growing black population never overtook the white citizenry, in power, privilege or size. At Hartsfield's urging, the city continually annexed, or tried to annex, neighboring white communities in an effort to maintain Atlanta's white majority.

Progress for African-Americans in Atlanta was negotiated step by step. In the late-1940s, the Auburn godfathers began pressing Hartsfield anew on their recurring demand that the city add African-American officers to the city's police force. Hartsfield had made excuses every time they had asked before, shrugging off complaints about the department's rampant brutality and hazardous indifference toward the black community. Only a few years earlier, he had even ignored the black veterans who marched from Ebenezer to City Hall to protest the city's continued refusal to hire black officers.

The mayor might have turned a deaf ear yet again had the Auburn Avenue men brought only their earnestness with them. But they had ammunition this time—the collective black vote—and they promised it to Hartsfield if he played his cards right.

The pledge was neither empty nor overblown. For two years, a coalition of black activists and interest groups—ministers, educators, the local NAACP, the To Improve Conditions Club, the Atlanta Urban League, Walden and Dobbs' Fulton County Citizens Democratic Club, black newspapers and radio programs – had waged a massive voter education and registration campaign while waiting for the Supreme Court of the United States to rule on a legal challenge to the state's whites-only primaries. Victory was a foregone conclusion, given that the high court had already outlawed whites-only elections in a Texas case. The coalition wanted to be ready when the court smacked the State of Georgia for continuing its discriminatory elections. In the interim, the group more than tripled black voter registration in the city.

The massive drive bore its first fruit in a 1946 special election to fill a vacated seat in the state's congressional delegation. Atlanta's black voters had tipped the scales in favor of Helen Douglas Mankin. Of the 17 contenders, she was the only one who had courted their vote and they rewarded her resoundingly.

Now, if William Hartsfield loved anything more than touting and growing his city, it was keeping his power. With a tough reelection bid of his own ahead of him, he recognized that the Auburn Avenue delegation had something he needed. At last, in 1947, he bowed to the long-running demand and promised to integrate the police department. But not without strings attached. One, the black officers could not patrol white neighborhoods. Two, they would not have authority to arrest white people. Three, they would have to be stationed somewhere other than the APD's downtown headquarters.

Even with those restrictions, the police union objected strenuously when the mayor and aldermen approved the hiring of eight black police officers. At the union's behest, a local court enjoined the city from desegregating the police force. But a higher court overturned the stay and on April 3, 1948, eight black men, all but one of them World War II veterans, reported for duty as new members of the Atlanta Police Department. In his re-election victory the following year, Hartsfield won the overwhelming majority of black votes.

Dobbs had despised the conditions attached to the black officers' hiring, but he accepted this incremental progress as a victory for Auburn

Avenue. Moreover, he knew the episode bode well for future demands, validating his long-held belief that the vote was the hammer African-Americans needed to break down barriers to their advancement. Besides, the Butler Street YMCA, already the locus of black leadership in Atlanta, would do just fine as the black officers' makeshift precinct.

Just around the corner from Auburn Avenue, the red brick, six-story Butler YMCA was a hive of political, economic, and social activity. On any given day, a visitor might spot the newly minted black lawmen adjusting their belts and badges before commencing the day's rounds. Once a month around noon one could witness a cluster of business types heading to a meeting of The Hungry Club, where politics and policy were served alongside the roast beef and potatoes. Occasionally, a couple of white men might show up for the club luncheon, skulking through the halls lest they draw too much attention and word reach downtown that they were there, mingling with Negroes. In another part of the YMCA, neighborhood youngsters like Vernon Jordan or Martin Luther King, Jr., could be found romping through the place, gearing up for a marble-shooting contest or a race in the swimming pool. And upstairs, the godfathers—and possibly a few influential women like community activist Ruby Blackburn and Urban League director Grace Towns Hamilton—would be plotting their next encounter with Hartsfield, the aldermen, the big-shot bankers, the white-shoe lawyers and the moneyed merchants who held the keys to things their people needed. There, the assembled guard would take yet another look at the numbers and scan reports from the field to make sure that the black vote, its coveted bargaining chip, was, like the city's black population itself, only getting bigger.

This was the Atlanta into which Michael Hollis was born in the fall of 1953. A city of stubborn segregation that yielded to neither moral suasion nor the national creed but insisted instead upon hoarding the lion's share of rights and privileges for its white citizens and meting out crumbs and morsels to others if and when it felt like it.

Michael was born on October 22 in a segregated wing of Grady Memorial Hospital. The house where four little children waited for their new baby brother to come home was on a segregated street in a segregated part of town. The public schools were segregated. The public library, public parks, public golf courses, tennis courts and swimming pools were segregated. The buses and trolley cars were segregated. So were theaters and restaurants and department stores, where his mother could select Easter outfits for his big brothers and sisters, but wouldn't be allowed to use the dressing rooms to make sure the clothing fit. In 1953, there were no blacks on the Atlanta Board of Aldermen, no blacks in the Georgia Legislature and no black judges. Black Atlantans could live only in those areas designated for Negroes by city ordinance, and their steadily increasing numbers meant most languished in crowded neighborhoods, in barebones houses or in decaying tenements where their children played on unpaved, unlit streets. Blacks were not allowed in the expansive, luxurious neighborhoods like Peyton Forest, Ansley Park, Morningside, Druid Hills and Buckhead unless they came as hired cooks, gardeners, drivers, nursemaids, handy-men or housecleaners.

For generations, the city had kept a tight lid on any ambitions that might one day emerge from black newborns like Michael. Granted, there had been encroachments, but for the most part, the age-old garrison of segregation, discrimination and privation was still holding fast in late 1953.

But change was coming. And Michael Hollis had arrived just in time to take part in it.

CHAPTER 3

Despite the cultural and institutional limitations that surrounded him, Michael was one of the fortunate ones. He was welcomed and wanted by his family. He was born to a nurturing mother who felt that there was something special about her youngest child from the beginning and took delight in the keen intellect and curiosity he exhibited even as a toddler. It saddened her that her children might not have all that they wanted or deserved. But as long as she was alive and able-bodied, Virginia Robinson Hollis would see to it that they would have what they needed. Not only would she provide for them, Mrs. Hollis resolved to teach her boys and girls how to seek and prepare for something better and to make the best of what they had in the meantime. She would be the one who kept them looking up, looking forward, thinking positively, remaining hopeful and prayerful and getting ready for what she assured them was an inevitable bounty of blessings. She would make certain the children never thought of themselves as poor, but instead, as abundantly blessed and loved.

Young Michael's father was more out of the picture than in it. Flem Hollis was a Pullman porter for the Norfolk Southern Railways, a job that kept him on the lines up and down the northeastern seaboard or on runs from Atlanta to New Orleans and back. By the time 36-year-old Flem met 22-year-old Virginia Robinson in 1947, he had been married, separated and widowed and was the father of a teenage son and daughter. Flem, Jr., often traveled with his father, living in boarding houses during the train crew's overnight stops, while Joan remained in Atlanta in a relative's care.

Flem, Sr., was smitten immediately by the lovely Virginia, mother to four-year-old James Bernard, and after a courtship closely monitored by Virginia's protective mother, the couple married in 1948 and moved themselves and their three children into a two-bedroom, one bath house on Joyce Street about five blocks from the Morehouse College campus.

Life for the little family quickly found its rhythm. Flem, Sr., would be gone for extended runs with the Norfolk Southern while Virginia held down a job as a waitress at the Busy Bee Cafe on Hunter Street and attended night school to learn bookkeeping and office management. Once the family started growing—starting with Julius' birth in 1950 and the rapid additions of Virginia Elaine in 1951, Ruth in 1952, and Michael in 1953—Mrs. Hollis found she could no longer do it all with five little ones, so for a while she gave up her job for full-time homemaking and motherhood.

Every now and then throughout the first decade of her marriage, word or evidence would surface that Flem, Sr., was not exactly behaving like a married man with seven children under wing. Virginia was plagued by rumors that her husband was fooling around with other women. That dishonor and his well-known affinity for gambling houses caused tension between the couple, already strained by the lengthy, frequent absences required by Flem's job. It didn't help either that he continually paid only lip service to Virginia's ongoing pleas to find a bigger house for the family.

Flem, Jr., served a stint in the U.S. Air Force, tooled around New York and, at his father's urging, returned to Atlanta and enrolled at Morris Brown College. While studying for a master's degree at Atlanta University, he fell in love with and married fellow student Dorothy Anderson, the beautiful, sweet-natured daughter of a South Carolina landowning family. Joan married her high school sweetheart, Sylvester Mitchell, and was building a family and a career in banking. But there were still five kids at home getting bigger by the day, requiring more and more space and privacy. Flem kept saying he was going to find them a bigger place, but he never did.

When Mrs. Hollis learned in the summer of 1957 that her husband was involved in a long-running affair with a local woman, just as rumor had it, it was the last straw. Flem arrived at their small house on Joyce Street one sunny summer afternoon to find his household packed up to move. A nasty argument ensued and quickly turned violent. Flem assaulted his wife, whose screams tore the children away from their neighborhood playmates and sent them barreling toward home only to find their mother under attack. Instinctively, they pounced on Flem "like a swarm of locusts," as Julius put it, and punched, bit, pulled and scratched their father until he left their mother alone and drove off.

Bloodied, swollen and bruised, Virginia was so frightened by the assault that she dispatched James Bernard, Julius and three-year-old Michael to live with her brother James and his wife, Pauline. The Robinsons warmly received their three nephews even though their household was already bursting at the seams with thirteen children—his, hers and theirs. Dear took Elaine and Ruth to her house and Virginia moved in temporarily with Leila Williams, her close friend and former co-worker at the Busy Bee who now had a diner of her own, Leila's Dinette. If Flem came back for another round of abuse, as Virginia thought he might, neither she nor her children would be there.

Nearly two months later, having had no sign of Flem and with a blue-chip divorce lawyer on her side—courtesy of Dear's sympathetic employers at the Druid Hills Golf Club—Virginia Hollis reunited her brood and the family completed their relocation to 1004 Joyce Street without incident. Dear moved in with them to provide perpetual assistance to her daughter and grandchildren. Once the divorce was finalized, Virginia went back to work, her wages augmented by court-ordered child support from Flem, who married Jeanette Johnson, the sister-in-law of Nathaniel Bronner, a founder of the famous Bronner Brothers hair products empire – a nation-wide business that had started modestly in 1947 with cosmetology classes and hair stylist shows at the Butler YMCA. Even though he earned good money on the railroad, it was not unusual for Flem to squander his earnings at the poker table. He sometimes fell behind in his monthly payments to the mother of his children, but the law would inevitably catch up with him and haul him downtown to shake the money loose. In one instance, the sheriff impounded the taxi he drove part-time until he made good on the arrearages.

"He was stunned and would stay embittered up until Michael turned eighteen years old," Julius said, recalling his father's resentment over the amount of child support he had to pay until his youngest child reached the age of majority.

Whether Flem appreciated it or not, his grudging contribution helped his ex-wife provide a more comfortable life for the Hollis children who, as teenagers, would take a certain sobering delight in the Temptations' hit song, "Papa Was a Rolling Stone." Ultimately, they moved to a larger and nicer home on West End Avenue even nearer to the Morehouse campus than before.

Michael thrived under the watchful eye of his doting mother and grandmother, and that of his sisters who, though barely older, tended to coddle and pamper him. On Sunday mornings, Dear and Virginia would see to it that everyone was fed and dressed for Sunday School at nearby Warner Memorial United Methodist Church. Hair combed, bows tied, belts buckled and dress shoes shined, the children would set out for church. Mrs. Hollis would arrive in time for the Eleven O'clock worship service.

"As soon as she came through that door, we knew to all go sit with her; three on this side, two on that side," says Elaine. "You didn't hear a peep out of us, either. We knew better."

Every other day would find Michael on the porch shortly before sunset, waiting for his mother's return from a day's work. Elaine remembers him bolting from the stoop when the city bus pulled up at the corner, discharging their weary mother.

"He would run all the way up the block, yelling, 'Movey's home,' and he'd hug her and help her carry her bag down the street, her holding one handle and him holding the other and they're just talking and laughing," she recalled. "She didn't slack any of us, but she and Michael just had that connection."

While Michael was hanging out with his sisters or Gregory, his one good friend in the neighborhood, his big brothers were indulging in stickball, touch football, foot races, and the occasional daredevil foolishness. Once, in an overzealous reenactment of the Wild Wild West, James Bernard and a friend took advantage of the younger Julius and strung him up from a tree branch near a retaining wall. Dear just happened to look out the kitchen window to see Julius dangling by his neck from the tree, the tips of his toes barely touching the wall and allowing just enough lift to avoid strangulation. She hurriedly got him down and sent right away for James Bernard and his friend who protested that they meant no harm and hadn't realized that Julius couldn't get down on his own—an excuse that did not spare either boy a good whipping.

Michael seldom joined in such rough-housing. Even after he was big enough to keep up with the older boys, he was more likely to be found with his head in a book, especially after that chance encounter with Dr. King at cousin Thelma's wedding. He was a hungry reader, devouring books, pamphlets and news articles about nonviolent resistance and social justice movements in India, China, and South Africa. That led him to conclude that economic empowerment was the key to social equality and that capitalism was the key to economic empowerment, a principle he would abide by for the rest of his life. Michael became so adept at the socio-economic sciences that, by the time Julius took his first economics course at Morehouse, he was ahead of his classmates, thanks to all of those nights he and his brother had debated Keynes, Friedman, and Samuelson's economic theories in the room they shared at home.

Michael's precocious fascination with such ponderous affairs was further fueled by his exposure to the movers and shakers who convened regularly at the Butler YMCA to discuss strategy and tactics for black advancement. Like many boys in the community, Michael was a regular at the Y. But while his peers came for the camaraderie and recreation, Michael's purpose was usually to pick the considerable brains of community heroes like Dr. Benjamin Mays, Morehouse's esteemed president, or John Cox, the Y's executive director and a man indubitably in-the-know when it came to politics and business. The men were apparently just as fascinated by the young boy philosopher as he was with them. They took him firmly under their wing.

Mrs. Hollis cherished her boy's inquisitiveness, his thirst for knowledge, his respect for elders and his appreciation for sage advice. In her view, God had placed men like Dr. Mays and John Cox in Michael's life to help her steer his gifts in the right direction. Lord knows, she was doing all she could to teach her children to reach higher. She had set the example by continuing her education at Reed Business School and parlaying her newly certified skills into a job as receptionist and scheduler for Dr. Harvey Smith, the popular dentist. Encouraged by his mother, Michael began dropping by her workplace to observe Dr. Smith and learn how he ran his business. They talked customer relations, marketing, inventory management, and regulatory compliance. They discussed how to prepare for a job interview, how to dress professionally, what to look for in employees, when to pay oneself, and the importance of putting money back into the business to sustain and grow it. Michael and Dr. Smith became so close and fond of one another that the busy, distinguished dentist had no compunction about acting as the occasional deliveryman for Michael's popular cake-selling business.

"One year, our mother gave a Monopoly game to Michael," Julius recalls. "He and James Bernard and I would play all day on Saturday and Sunday into the night. Michael mastered it. I think it gave him his first insight into strategy and negotiating."

Michael reached tenth grade in 1968, having never had a white classmate. Indeed, he never would throughout his secondary education. Atlanta's public high schools had been desegregated since 1961, seven years after the Supreme Court neutered the insidious separate-but-equal doctrine of public education; and six years after the Supremes ordered the nation's public schools to desegregate "with all deliberate speed."

Atlanta's white establishment had been rattled by the violence that had greeted school desegregation efforts in other southern cities like Little

Rock and New Orleans. They worried that Atlanta might suffer the same fate and fretted over the unrest and white flight that would ensue if the city's black and white schoolchildren were forced to learn and play together. As white Atlantans recoiled from the *Brown v. Board* decision, school districts throughout the state deployed a series of tactics to delay the inevitable, all the while looking for loopholes that might allow their rabble-rousing governor to keep his word that "none, not one" black child would ever be enrolled in a white public school in Georgia. Ever the cunning sales-man, Mayor Hartsfield used this period of limbo to re-brand Atlanta as "The City Too Busy to Hate"—a slogan that honest constituents knew to be delusional.

Michael blossomed at Booker T. Washington High School, Atlanta's first public high school for blacks and a source of great pride in the African-American community. The school's construction in 1924 had been a mile-stone in the city's racial politics, a magnificent memento of the time black voters triumphed over white resistance and effectively forced the city to acknowledge that black children deserved more than nine years of formal education. For students, parents and educators alike, Washington High was both a storehouse and exhibit hall for black pride and achievement, replete with a rigorous curriculum and talented, dedicated educators, many of them Morehouse and Spelman graduates.

Michael took full advantage of the opportunity. Not only did he get involved in student government, but through his connections at "the black city hall," he became engaged in grown-up governance too. John Cox had piqued his protégé's interest in city politics and, before his freshman year was over, Michael plunged in to help a dashing newcomer on the Atlanta political scene—Maynard Jackson, Jr., who was running for vice mayor.

Besides a degree from Morehouse and a license to practice law, Jackson came from a respected family of high achievers. His late father had been a pastor at Friendship Baptist Church, the birthplace of Morehouse College; his mother held a Master's in French from the University of Toulouse in France and taught at Spelman; one of his maternal aunts, Mattiwilda Dobbs, was an internationally acclaimed opera star, the first black person to sing at Milan's celebrated La Scala opera house and a performer with the Metropolitan Opera. Most importantly for a black political novice in Atlanta at that time, Maynard was the grandson of none other than the late Mayor of Sweet Auburn, John Wesley Dobbs, his mother's father.

Despite Maynard's impressive pedigree, the black leadership at the Butler Y had not looked kindly upon his quixotic attempt to unseat long-time incumbent Herman Talmadge in the U.S. Senate race of 1968. An inexperienced upstart taking on one of the state's most seasoned, powerful pols was not what the Auburn Avenue decision-makers had in mind for breaking the white man's exclusive hold on elected office. And the timing was off. They had marked the 1977 city elections as their target for putting up a black candidate for office—a candidate they would recruit, vet and prepare; someone they knew, like Leroy Johnson, Georgia's first black legislator since Reconstruction; or Vernon Jordan of the Southern Regional Council. Maynard was not on their radar screens and had not even consulted them, let alone sought their blessing to run for office. As far as the godfathers were concerned, his candidacy was a fool's errand. Though they knew what was coming, the old men of Auburn Avenue could not have been happy to be proven right on Election Day when Talmadge not only won re-election but trounced Jackson in the process. To Jackson's astonishment, Talmadge had won a heap of black votes.

Maynard later said that, realistically, he hadn't expected to win, but believed that an unrepentant segregationist like Talmadge should not go unchallenged. Michael liked that about him, just as he admired Jackson's willingness to plunge into a recent disturbance at Morehouse involving a band of students and the Board of Trustees – a protest that involved sophomore Samuel L. Jackson, the future actor, and a band of one hundred or more other Morehouse students, including Michael's brother, Julius.

Upset that their demands for Afrocentric courses and more blacks on the board had gone unheeded, the students commandeered a board meeting and locked the distinguished Morehouse trustees in the building for two days. Jackson, siding with the students, helped broker a settlement to bring the disorder to an end.

The Morehouse takeover was part of a new wave of political tactics in the city, ushered in by a troop of well-educated and insistent young black men and women who had lost patience with the old guard's negotiate-and-litigate methodology. To the shock and dismay of Auburn Avenue, the young Turks practiced confrontation— "direct action," in the parlance of civil disobedience—to get attention for their movement and to pressure their targets into prompt and dramatic change rather than the gradualism of the past. There had been only glimpses of such pressure politics before.

With rare effrontery, a group of black ministers had done something bold in the late 1950s when they boarded city buses and trolleys and refused to sit in the back or to surrender their seats to white passengers as the law required. It took a couple of years, but that act of defiance led to the desegregation of Atlanta's public transportation system. Similarly, Mrs. Irene Dobbs Jackson—Maynard's mother—had strolled into the segregated main branch of the Atlanta Public Library one day in 1959, requesting a library card and she walked out with one, thereby erasing the color line at the facility. Throughout the early 1960s, acts of civil disobedience—non-violent and dignified each time—toppled old barriers. Public golf courses, tennis courts, parks, swimming pools and theaters were desegregated, though whites often abandoned the facilities afterward rather than bow to the new order.

Still, the city had never before seen the likes of the Committee on Appeal for Human Rights (COAHR), a coalition of students from Atlanta's black universities including Julian Bond, Lonnie King, Mary Ann Smith, James Felder, Don Clark, Roslyn Pope, Herschelle Sullivan, Carolyn Long, Marian Wright and others. Over the objections of the black community's elder statesmen, COAHR staged sit-ins at segregated lunch counters, protest marches at downtown establishments, and in 1960, the boycott of nearly 70 downtown Atlanta stores. For months, employees, customers, and passersby had to weave around picketers at popular retail establishments like Rich's, a marquee department store that catered to the well-to-do of any race and, unusually, extended charging privileges to black customers. "Close down your account with segregation; open up your account with freedom" was the demonstrators' running chant.

At first, the old guard on Auburn Avenue balked. Public demonstrations were not its way of doing business. The godfathers had always operated behind the scenes, relying on carefully crafted compromises and quid pro quo to get what they wanted from the established powers. Several university presidents pleaded with the students to abandon their confrontational tactics, arguing that black dignity and safety were at stake, but to no avail.

It took the arrest of demonstrator Martin Luther King, Jr., to change the older men's tune. After King was moved from the city jail to Reidsville Prison on the pretext that he had failed to convert his valid Alabama driver's license into a Georgia license, they too put on their marching shoes and joined the ring of protestors pounding the pavement outside Rich's entrance.

That act of solidarity aside, tension remained between the old and new factions, and it came to a head when 2,000 people gathered at Warren Memorial, the Hollis family's home church, on March 10, 1961. Only days before, the old guard had struck an agreement with downtown merchants to end the protests in exchange for desegregating the stores. These changes were to coincide with the desegregation of the Atlanta public schools at summer's end. The new guard of young activists fumed about the bargain.

For one thing, they had not been involved in the deal-making and for another, the agreement sounded like a set up for a sucker punch. The deal smacked of pacification, COAHR argued, and there was no way to enforce the merchants' end of the bargain. As the meeting grew more and more contentious, tempers flared and a few of the young activists berated the Auburn Avenue men as "Uncle Toms" and "sellouts." Some of the elders barked back, most notably Rev. Martin King, Sr., who bellowed to one young critic, "Boy, I'm sick of you."

It took the softly spoken, studied calm of Martin King, Jr., to break the stalemate. King called for solidarity between the two factions even while acknowledging that the controversial agreement was flawed, containing no guarantees that the white businessmen would keep their word and no consequences if they didn't. It came down to integrity, King said. "If anyone fails to keep his word," he advised, "let it be the white man."

The agreement was signed and, to the activists' relief, the month after nine black students began classes at four of the city's previously all-white public high schools on August 30, 1961, downtown merchants opened their cafeterias, dressing rooms and restrooms to all customers, regardless of race.

The old style of managing racial politics—the "Atlanta Way"—had prevailed once again, but everyone knew its days were numbered. A less patient and more theatrical approach to civil rights, engineered by feisty, well-educated young people, was taking over. Michael, then 15 years old, identified with the politically daring generation and its sometimes brazen, unapologetic approach to claiming its due. Although Maynard Jackson was not a demonstrator, he clearly belonged to the new wave of community activists and Michael liked the man's intelligence, independence, self-confidence, and energy. He especially admired Jackson's get-back-on-the-horse mentality since he was cut from the same cloth. Michael loved that Jackson had been so undaunted by the loss to Talmadge that the very next year, he announced his candidacy for the vice mayoralty of Atlanta, the ex officio president of the Board of Aldermen and a vantage for higher office.

Once again, Jackson had not courted the godfathers' approval or advice. This time, however, he won, thanks to solid support from black voters and the tireless campaign efforts of operatives like "Young Atlantans for Maynard Jackson," the volunteer group to which Michael belonged. The victory made Jackson only the second black person since the late 1800's to win election to a city office in Atlanta. Q.V. Williamson had broken through four years prior, winning a seat on the Board of Aldermen.

Michael's friendship with the new vice mayor, his enthusiasm for civic affairs and his conspicuous smarts made him a natural choice for appointment to Atlanta's Youth Congress, an auxiliary of city government aimed at fostering civic education and involvement among the city's young people. Elected president of the Youth Congress, Michael became the so-called "night mayor" of Atlanta, fielding constituents' after-hours phone calls and reporting back to Mayor Sam Massell, the relatively progressive new mayor who had been swept into office with a nod from Auburn Avenue and the solid support of black voters even though a respected black educator and reformer, Howard Tate, had sought the post.

Michael's prestigious appointment put him in touch with many of the other powerful folks at City Hall and afforded him a first-hand look at the machinery of city government. As always, his outgoing personality and obvious intelligence won the notice and favor of the City Hall fathers and, upon meeting them, he made a point of gathering phone numbers and filing them away in the event he needed them some day. Building, maintaining and using a network of powerful and connected people would be a major component of Michael Hollis' success strategy throughout his life. As Maynard Jackson once noted, "Michael remembers names and follows up on contacts like no one I've seen in my life."

One month before his graduation from Washington High in 1971, Michael traveled to Estes Park, Colorado, as a delegate to the White House Conference on Youth and Families. He had been nominated by the governor and appointed by President Nixon. When he graduated from Washington High, everyone expected him to enroll at Morehouse in the fall of 1971 since his brothers had studied there, one of his most respected mentors was the school's president, Morehouse was not only in his hometown but in his neighborhood, and it was nationally acclaimed for its scholastic heft.

But Michael had another plan. He wanted to go to a school that would widen his circle of influential friends and broaden his experience. He was also mindful of Dr. Mays' lamentations about the racist limitations imposed on his own options when he was college-bound and Michael considered how he might avenge that injustice by doing what the brilliant Dr. Mays could not do: matriculate in the Ivy League. Thus, to many people's surprise, and disappointment in some cases, Michael announced that he had chosen Dartmouth College for his undergraduate studies.

For the first time in his life, he would be living somewhere other than Atlanta. He could not have chosen a place more different than western New Hampshire.

CHAPTER 4

Michael arrived in Hanover, New Hampshire, just as the leaves on the ubiquitous hardwoods were poised to present their annual extravaganza of yellow, orange and red. The rolling hills of the Upper Connecticut River Valley draped the pastoral campus of Dartmouth College, the town's centerpiece and point of pride with its Georgian-style architecture, curved walkways, and clustered dormitory buildings fanning out from "The Green," a huge, open expanse that often doubles as a staging ground for many of the town's festivals. He would have found the Dartmouth campus beautiful, placid and stately. And very, very white.

For the black college-bound, the coincidence of federal civil rights legislation and the recommendations of the National Advisory Commission on Civil Disorders (a.k.a., the Kerner Commission Report), had opened the doors, if not the hearts and minds, of theretofore all-white or overwhelmingly white colleges and universities across the country. In the name of equal opportunity, state-funded institutions were forced to comply, however resentfully, since African-American tax dollars were carrying part of their load. Many private institutions had been enrolling and graduating African-American students since long before the Civil War, but black students at America's most prestigious institutions of higher learning were still relatively few and far between more than a century later. Whether for reasons of conscience or competition, private institutions stepped up the pace in the late 1960s so that by the time Michael arrived at Dartmouth in September 1971, there were about three hundred black students enrolled there—not even a tenth of total enrollment, but still, the most Dartmouth had ever had. All of them were men, as Dartmouth would not go co-ed until the following year, the last Ivy League sister to do so.

Hanover had a population of about ten thousand—a tiny place in Michael's eyes. Atlanta lost that many white people to the suburbs every year. Like Michael, most of Dartmouth's African-American students were from large metropolises like Chicago, Los Angles, New York and Houston—places with significant black populations. A town as small as Hanover was one thing for them to get used to; the overwhelming white-ness of their new environment was quite another. Little wonder then that the black students tended to stick together, enjoying fellowship in Cutter Hall, home of the Afro-American Society – a social and cultural group that had been founded as a meeting place, resource center and dormitory for black undergrads. The awkward co-existence between black and white students occasionally erupted into a confrontation, but for the most part, an interracial truce prevailed on the bucolic campus.

When they could, Michael and his friends would escape the confines of Hanover for brief junkets to large, urban, driving-distance destinations like Boston, where clubs, restaurants and women—and more than a handful of black folks—could be found. Get-a-ways required someone with a vehicle and a willingness to drive a couple of hours each way with a carload of excited, or exhausted, classmates. Michael sometimes made the trips, but as that first year wore on, he more often than not remained behind, spending his downtime having dinner with professors. It was almost as if he considered the highly accomplished faculty members and administrators more on his level than his true peers. His classmates may have thought so too. Maybe that's why they called him "the governor."

Benjamin Wilson was a junior at Dartmouth when Michael arrived and recalls an engagingly brash young man.

"He was going to be the next mayor of Atlanta," recalls Wilson, now a prominent environmental attorney in Washington, D.C. "He was this very bright, precocious, can-do kind of guy. He organized an investment club at Dartmouth. So, even in college, he had a big vision."

Dr. Leroy Keith, Jr., then an associate dean and assistant professor at the college, recalls first meeting Michael as classes got underway in 1971.

"I'm walking across the campus of Dartmouth College. This young man approached me and he looked me straight in the eye and said, 'My name is Michael Hollis. I am from Atlanta, Georgia, and I am a graduate of Booker T. Washington High School.'"

Impressed by Michael's boldness and initiative, Keith, a Morehouse man (and, later, president of Morehouse), became an instant fan of the young student and soon became yet another of Michael's trusted mentors, commencing a friendship that would last for the rest of Michael's life. As the educator quickly learned, Michael had never been just another face in the crowd back home in Atlanta and he wasn't about to merely blend in at Dartmouth, never mind that the place was foreign to all he had ever known.

"He cut a swath through Dartmouth College during his freshman year," said Dr. Keith, "and became well-known for his academic and leadership ability."

The weekend dinners with professors were one reason for "the governor's" renown on campus. Another was his habit of spending hours upon hours at Parkhurst Hall in the president's office and those of other top school officials, who all came to understand that the smart, confident and nakedly ambitious first-year student was one to watch. For example, near the end of his freshman year, when he learned that black alumni were planning a first-ever conference on campus, Michael decided he wanted a role in it and informed Dr. Keith, who was advising the group, that he would like to introduce the event's keynote speaker.

"The night of the banquet, Michael gave a twenty-minute introduction," Dr. Keith recalled. "He got a standing ovation. The speaker didn't."

Michael's rousing speech and the crowd's reaction to it apparently made Dartmouth's president take another look at the young man he had already come to know as a fixture at Parkhurst Hall. Soon after the black alumni conference, he invited Michael to serve as his administrative intern for the coming school term, a coveted position that made the chosen one the president's liaison to the student body and vice versa.

Naturally, Michael leaped at the opportunity. Being selected by the college president to serve as his eyes and ears on the ground was high honor enough. But President Kemeny was someone Michael honestly respected and admired and he looked forward to getting to know the president better.

A Hungarian-born Jew, John George Kemeny and his family had immigrated to America in 1940 to escape Nazi atrocities. He excelled in school, won admission to Princeton University and, while still a student there, worked on the Manhattan Project, the U.S.-led research and development of nuclear weapons. He returned to Princeton to complete his studies in mathematics and philosophy and enrolled in graduate school—assisting world-famous physicist Albert Einstein in the process—and earned his doctorate in 1949. After two years in the mathematics department at Dartmouth, Kemeny was named department chair. In 1964, he and a colleague invented BASIC, the programming language that allowed ordinary people to use computers.

Kemeny had ascended the presidency of Dartmouth only one year before Michael's arrival, but he had already established a reputation as a change agent, remodeling old systems so that the school could accommodate more students without expanding facilities—the vaunted "Dartmouth Plan" of year-round classes. He also increased the numbers of students and faculty of color, attracted more international students, and opened enrollment to female students. And he still taught two classes each year.

Michael liked men of action and accomplishment like Kemeny and fancied himself as one of them. He also liked that Kemeny followed his own conscience, rather than bandwagon politics, as exemplified in the president's decision to cancel classes for a week and host a day of mourning and "soul searching" the day after the Ohio National Guard gunned down four anti-war protestors at Kent State on May 4, 1970. Kemeny had only been president for two months at the time and his reaction to the Kent killings rankled conservative city leaders and alumni. He stood his ground even as the staunchly conservative editorialists of the *Manchester Union-Leader* derided his decision under a headline that read, "Dartmouth Picks a Lemon."

Michael's admiration of Dr. Kemeny was reciprocated and not by just the president. In her 1979 memoir, *It's Different at Dartmouth*, Jean Alexander Kemeny, the president's wife, wrote glowingly of Michael, who served an unprecedented two-year stint as the president's administrative intern.

"He had a special gift: equal rapport with blacks and whites," wrote Mrs. Kemeny. "And he could give an invocation or speech that would knock you out of your chair – a young Martin Luther King."

For those who knew Michael, the Dartmouth first lady's flattering assessment was no exaggeration. Though well aware of his hometown's racial history and quite serious about stamping out discrimination, Michael exuded a confident nonchalance about other people's bigotry when faced with it personally. Racist sentiments were the ignoramus' problem, not his. Instead, he focused on making mincemeat of their prejudices and presumptions, enabled by a powerful intellect, his mother's lessons and the signature tenet of his esteemed mentor, Dr. Benjamin Mays, who regularly counseled black people to "never accept subservience and segregation in their own minds."

In addition to his studies and consuming obligations as the president's intern, Michael was active in the Afro-American Society, led a group that was responsible for bringing top public speakers to campus, and was the custodian of the files on Dartmouth's extensive permanent art collection. Taking advantage of his soothing, baritone voice, he also was a DJ and sports announcer for the college radio station, WDCR.

"Michael Hollis was the big man on campus, no question about it," said Gary Love, a Chicago native who came to Dartmouth in 1972. "He was brilliant and his articulation of issues in the world was a step ahead of most of us. Michael was playing chess when all of us were playing checkers."

It was at a gathering of the Afro-American Society that Love first encountered Michael. "He was in full regalia, talking and holding court and I was intrigued by him. He was the guy who commanded an audience." Love also recalls Michael's voracious appetite for reading and his long recall of book passages and news articles he had read years before.

"He had a view of the world going into Dartmouth that most of us didn't have until our business years," says Love. "He knew that relationships were key. He always remembered a name and a face. He knew how to work it."

Love happily fell into Michael's orbit, sharing his interest in politics, which Michael continued to cultivate despite his many preoccupations at Dartmouth.

A foundation scholarship and financial aid were paying for Michael's education, but money was otherwise often tight and he usually was able to get back to Atlanta only twice a year—at Christmas break and at school year's end. He spent most other holidays with the Kemenys and their two children or with other prominent people he had befriended in town. Still, he kept in constant touch with his mother, other family members and friends back home, making a habit of checking in regularly with John Cox at the Butler Y, still the headquarters of Atlanta's black business and political life.

Things were cracking back home. The city, now predominantly black, was bursting with change—revolution, actually. After four years as vice mayor, Maynard Jackson, Michael's mentor and patron, had been elected mayor of Atlanta, walloping Sam Massell, who was seeking a second term. For the first time ever, a major Southern city had an African-American at the helm of government. That would not be the only mark Maynard Jackson left on history.

As with his first two attempts at elected office, Jackson met resistance from the black leadership at the Butler Y when he announced his mayoral candidacy in early 1973. Once again, the dazzling young politico had usurped the old guard and without so much as a nod to its plan to introduce a black mayoral candidate in 1977, when Mayor Massell would have completed two terms.

"I have come to my decision, in large part, because so many of you have urged me to run; so many of you who come from all walks of life, who come from every corner of our great city, and who represent every racial, religious, economic and age group," Jackson said at the City Hall news conference where he announced his candidacy.

For sure, the godfathers had not been among those urging a Jackson candidacy. With Maynard jumping ahead of their schedule, they ached to reassert their power and deliver a chastening message to Jackson, which they did by positioning state Senator Leroy Johnson for the mayor's race. Despite the heady sponsorship of powerful men like A.T. Walden and other Butler Y habitués, the popular and experienced Johnson never fared well in the race. At a mock election at Morehouse following appearances by Jackson and Johnson, the vice mayor thrashed the state senator, who would go on to win less than four percent of the vote in the real election.

Out of a field of twelve candidates, only Jackson and Massell were left standing after the October 1973 election. Massell knew his hold on the black vote was shaky this time, but he hoped the old black leadership and a bloc of black votes would come through for him in the November runoff the way it had when he first ran in 1969. Back then, Massell had attracted black voters with promises to increase the number of African-American employees in city government and a certain social kinship as a Jewish man whose ethnic group had not always been welcome in WASP society. He was counting on black leadership to wait until 1977 before backing a black candidate for the city's top post, as agreed.

But three things foiled Massell. One was his handling of a sanitation strike in 1970. Massell had opposed demands for higher wages and fired one thousand workers. Jackson, the outspoken vice mayor, made hay of the mayor's resistance, publicly condemning him.

Massell's second mistake was his oft-expressed dread of a black majority in Atlanta – a stance that Jackson lambasted repeatedly – and his fondness for annexation, that tried-and-true tactic of white empowerment in Atlanta and a pet gambit among local politicians. In his quest to ward off a black majority, William Hartsfield had successfully led the charge to annex all-white suburban communities in 1952. Now, it was Massell's turn at the tactic. In his urgency to expand the city limits and swallow up more white citizens, Massell astonished a black audience by advising it to "think white" and help him secure a white majority population to save the city. The scorn heaped upon Massell for those patently offensive remarks deeply wounded his relationship with black leaders.

But the final blow to Massell's popularity among black Atlantans was his appointment of John Inman, his brother's drinking buddy, as chief of police. Inman lorded over a predominantly white department that was notorious for indignities, brutalities and discrimination against Atlanta's black residents – complaints the chief routinely ignored. His men rewarded his indifference with unyielding loyalty to their chief, all the while continuing their violence and harassment of the black citizenry. Time and again,

Mayor Massell stood by Chief Inman, who only flaunted his unchecked power all the more with each shrug of the official shoulder.

Massell's turpitude was reminiscent of another Atlanta mayor who had once enjoyed widespread black support, only to blow it with a preposterous, tin-eared blunder.

Ivan Allen, Jr., Massell's predecessor, had won over black support with his acceptance of school desegregation, his efforts to keep the peace between blacks and whites during the height of demonstrations against downtown merchants, and his testimony in support of civil rights legislation at a congressional hearing where he had been the only southern elected official to speak in favor of the bill. It was also Allen who ordered the "white" and "colored" signs removed from City Hall.

But, in December 1962, white homeowners in the affluent Cascade Heights subdivision rebelled when a black doctor and his family moved into their neighborhood, decrying the black family as intruders. Allen appeased the white homeowners by hastily erecting barricades on Peyton and Harlan Roads to discourage other African-Americans from stepping over the color line and settling in Cascade Heights. Black Atlantans and progressives were outraged over Allen's "Berlin Wall" and took the matter to court, where installation of the barricades was ruled unconstitutional. Allen had the barriers removed within minutes of the judge's decision, but his favorable reputation among Atlanta's black citizens was critically and permanently wounded.

* * *

Once it was clear that he had squandered his black support and that Maynard Jackson's candidacy was gaining momentum, Massell turned to scaremongering to whip up white voter trepidation and turnout. Repeatedly, he insinuated that a Jackson victory would lead to black dominance in city government and that, in turn, would sound Atlanta's death knell. To underscore that position, he sponsored an astonishingly dystopian campaign advertisement that dripped with racial innuendo. Aired on television and splayed in newspapers, the ad featured a dark, grossly littered, foreboding city street with the caption, "Atlanta's Too Young to Die"—a dog whistle to those who feared black majority rule.

Yet, the black electorate's hardening opposition to another Massell term did not necessarily redound to Jackson's benefit. Within the black power base, there were still plenty of sore feelings over Maynard's disregard for its authority, agenda and timetable. Black leaders still had serious reservations about Jackson's readiness for the job and his intentions. As disgusted as they were with Massell's shenanigans, they remained reticent to join the vice mayor's camp until they came face-to-face with redoubtable evidence that Jackson's candidacy had legs – a revelation uncovered by two polls commissioned by Maynard's close advisor, David Franklin.

One showed that Jackson would not only handily defeat any of his many opponents in the mayor's race, but that he would demolish Massell in a head-to-head contest. Contrary to the opposition's determined efforts to paint Jackson as a fire-breathing extremist, the second poll revealed that the majority of white voters did not consider him too radical for their taste.

A surprised but persuaded Jesse Hill, Jr., the president and CEO of Alonzo Herndon's Atlanta Life Insurance Company, took the poll results to his fellow black business leaders and convinced them that, as a matter of practicality, Jackson was their man. Thus did Maynard Jackson at last win over the old guard.

From his station eleven hundred miles away, Michael kept his hand in Jackson's race as much as he could, consulting with campaign workers and cashing in political chits for the sake of Maynard's candidacy. Every week, he spent hours on the phone discussing tactics and strategy with his brother Julius, who was working in the district offices of Congressman Andrew Young and, like Michael, pitching in where he could to help Jackson. Both rejoiced when Maynard won the runoff in November 1973, and watched in awe as their friend took the city by storm, thanks in part to a revamped city government charter chiefly designed by the president of the Atlanta Urban League, the brilliant Grace Hamilton Towns. Not only did the new charter bestow more unilateral authority upon the Office of Mayor, it also replaced the all at-large Board of Aldermen with a City Council of 18 members, two-thirds of whom would be elected by district and the remainder at-large. For the first time ever, black Atlantans had significant representation on the entity that called the shots in their city. Half of the official city fathers were black.

Almost immediately, Jackson sent shock waves through the white business community by announcing that the large, delectable pie of opportunity that had sated their ambitions and sugared their pockets would thenceforth be shared with black businesses or else the pie would be no more. He decreed that twenty-five percent of all city contracts were to be awarded to African-American entrepreneurs, a fifty-fold increase over the paltry rate of "minority" contracting when he took office. The twenty-five percent baseline was later codified in a 1975 city ordinance sponsored by Morris Finley, one of Jackson's many confreres on the City Council. The Finley Ordinance had a huge impact on Atlanta's banking community, where Jackson threatened to withdraw $600 million in city assets from banks that had no black officers or executives and move the accounts to those that did. Suddenly, banks in Atlanta began hiring African-American managers. Michael's half-sister, Joan Hollis Mitchell, was the first black woman bank officer in the city.

Nowhere did the Finley Ordinance have a more profound and norm-shattering effect than at Hartsfield International, the city's burgeoning airport named for the mayor who had turned an old auto racing strip into a major hub of commercial aviation. The massive $400 million expansion project would transform the airport into the city's supreme economic force, but it had languished for a decade, bogged down by indecision and red tape. Jackson was determined to kick-start it, but with a proviso. He voided all existing contracts and ordered that new bids be taken for every facet of the project, from terminal architecture and runway construction to retail outlets and custodial services, in accordance with his twenty-five percent mandate.

"We simply won't build it if you don't agree to this," Jackson famously said to appalled white business leaders. "You can have 75 percent of the project or you can have 100 percent of nothing. What is your choice?"

Jackson devised a joint venture program that allowed white and black firms to partner, if that's what it took to meet his unnegotiable diversity criteria. The mayor's method drew lawsuits, public harangues, and accusations of racism and favoritism, but it survived every test and scores of black businesses seized the new opportunities that the mayor had unleashed.

"It's very hard looking back now to believe that we were so naïve as to believe that we would be applauded by taking positive steps to go out and include rather than exclude American citizens from the government," said Emma Darnell, Jackson's Commissioner of Administration Services, in a 1988 interview for Henry Hampton's award-winning "Eyes on the Prize" project. "We were shocked and we were surprised not only about the intensity of the opposition which we received from the business community—certain elements of the business community and from certain contractors who had become rich at the city's expense."

For the rest of his life, Jackson would gloat over the fact that the giant airport project was completed "ahead of schedule and under budget," embarrassing skeptics and vindicating his affirmative action and joint venture initiatives.

Although he had yet to conceive Air Atlanta, Michael understood that the ground had been plowed and readied for his eventual return home and for the triumphant business life he had already envisioned for himself.

First, however, he had to complete his preparation, so Michael took full advantage of all that Dartmouth had to offer. He distinguished himself in classes and studied abroad in France and Sierra Leone as part of the school's academic exchange program. In his junior year, he took the lead in arranging several sit-downs between Dartmouth officials and a fellow Georgian who had announced his intention to run for president of the United States in 1976. Once the Dartmouth meetings were done, Michael accompanied his guest to gatherings with other prominent people in the Granite State. Thus, it was Michael Hollis who introduced James Earl Carter to the nation's first presidential primary state at a time when much of the country was still referring to the Georgia governor as "Jimmy Who."

In his final year at Dartmouth, Michael didn't attend classes because he didn't have to. He was one of only a dozen students selected for the senior fellowship program in the 1974-75 term, spending his last year on an independent study project in which he analyzed the political climate surrounding the creation of rapid transit systems in San Francisco and Atlanta. He also used his high stature on campus to turn a favor for his old mentor, Dr. Benjamin Mays. In 1975, Michael led efforts to confer an honorary doctorate degree from Dartmouth College upon Dr. Mays, fulfilling the distinguished educator's long-lost dream of attaching to the Ivy League.

In her paean to Dartmouth, Jean Kemeny recounts a prophecy made to her husband by Reg Murphy, the venerated editor of the *Atlanta Constitution*: "Do you know that you have the first black president of the United States at Dartmouth? His name is Michael Hollis—and he's a freshman." According to Mrs. Kemeny, Murphy told her husband that Michael had such a promising future in politics that Maynard Jackson had once quipped that he had better hurry and run for mayor before Michael graduated. Murphy had previously published an editorial when Michael was barely out of his teens, lauding him as "black, smart, ambitious, worldly beyond his years" and advising readers to "mark his name down" because "Mike Hollis may well be standing before this nation describing his vision of what it could become...."

"When Mike reaches that pinnacle – and he will," wrote Mrs. Kemeny of Michael's presidential potential, "I'll vote for him. His qualities are many, but two are rare: a true sense of his own worth and a special sweetness."

Whether they experienced that "special sweetness" or not, no one who ever met him doubted that Michael knew who he was, understood his value and had not only dreams of reaching the pinnacle of success but a map for getting there.

CHAPTER 5

The Michael Hollis Game Plan for Success included law school. At age 12, he had declared to his family that he intended to be a lawyer. Nine years later, with a bachelor's degree from Dartmouth College in hand, he was ready to make good on that vow.

Harvard, Yale, and Emory had been on the table as possibilities, but he couldn't stop thinking about the University of Virginia Law School and the fact that both Robert and Ted Kennedy had earned their degrees there in the 1950s. He figured that if he was ever to have a career in politics—and he was seriously considering it—then following in the footsteps of two princes of American politics—not to mention a legion of U.S. senators, congressmen, governors and federal judges—would only add luster to any future candidacy.

"In deciding on a legal career, I honestly feel that it is through this profession that I can give my best to my people and to my country," Michael had written in the personal statement required of applicants. "I want to enter law school and learn the fundamentals of law. I want to be able to say what Elliot Richardson said to the former president—"No"—when asked by politicians and other public administrators to do something to which I conscientiously object.

"Furthermore, having a legal training will give me the kinds of options that I think will be helpful to me if I embark on a public career. I am concerned about the future of our cities—the influence of mass transit, the role of the arts in reshaping and influencing growth and development, and the kinds of pressures that are brought to bear with the changing racial make-up of our urban areas."

The summer before he started law school, Michael made a trip to New York City to secure funding for his legal education from the Leopold Schepp Foundation, a 50-year-old philanthropic organization. Named for a German-American who had to quit school as a child to work and help support his widowed mother only to reach adulthood and become a successful Manhattan businessman, the foundation was initially established to "encourage young people to develop good character and to help them complete their high school education." Once high school became obligatory, the Schepp Foundation shifted its focus to college and graduate school applicants, emphasizing character, academic ability, and financial need. Only a small portion of the foundation's largesse was allotted for medical, law and business students. Michael was one of the lucky few to win a scholarship for law school.

As at Dartmouth, Michael found a beautiful, spacious and ver-dant campus at the University of Virginia, adorned with classic, historic architecture. Like Dartmouth was to Hanover, UVA was the focal point of Charlottesville, which was absorbed in preparations for the nation's bicen-tennial celebration when Michael arrived in the fall of 1975.

Charlottesville had more than four times the population of Hanover, but it was still much smaller than Atlanta – ten times smaller, in fact. Still, Michael found remarkable similarities. After all, like his hometown, Charlottesville was part of the Old South, the land of slow, lilting accents; rich, rib-sticking food; fragrant, flowering trees; and old-fashioned eti-quette. Of course, it also was home to banal dispositions about race and gender, hidebound traditions and a lingering resentment over the demise of the Confederacy whose capital, Richmond, was a mere 70 miles down the road from the UVA campus.

Once again, Michael had chosen to pursue a degree at a historic, prestigious institution in an overwhelmingly white environment. He was one of about a dozen black students in the freshman class that year. But, he kept his eye on the end game – the payoffs that came with hailing from one of the country's oldest and foremost law schools. Besides, he knew how to navigate those familiar waters; he had a lifetime of training and testing. Racial antagonism had never crimped his style before and it wouldn't now.

Which is why, on the very first day of classes at UVA, Dan Kolber found his fellow first-year student in the midst of a heated argument in the hallway. Inveterately curious, Kolber sauntered over to listen in on what seemed to him like some kind of interracial showdown.

Kolber was no stranger to racial politics, having grown up in Coral Gables, Florida, about 20 miles south of Miami, during a time when black people were generally consigned to the most menial jobs, the poorest neighborhoods and the neediest schools and middle class Jewish families like his were barred from certain residential areas and businesses.

"I was reading the *Miami Herald* daily by the time I was eight years old and became acutely aware of the bigotry in south Florida," Dan recalled. "Blacks were not allowed on the streets at night on Miami Beach. Hotels would have signs that said, 'No Jews.'"

Kolber had a bachelor's degree from Boston University, where he had been lured by the school's reputation as a center of social activism, in particular, its student and faculty opposition to the raging Vietnam War. At BU, he had fallen under the high-minded spell of Dr. Howard Zinn, the historian and archangel of socio-political academia whose eventual award-winning magnum opus, *A People's History of the United States*, would become required reading at schools nationwide. Dan had always questioned the establishment, the status quo, and conventional wisdom. His time at Boston University, a citadel of progressive thought, sealed his decidedly liberal bent. As a champion debater and accomplished scholar, Kolber had been wooed by the university's law school, but he wanted to look at other top law schools in the U.S., and chose UVA because he had promised himself he would enroll in the best school that accepted him.

"There was an argument going on in the hallway, literally the first day of law school," Kolber recalled. "And I come over and there was Michael arguing with these right-wingers. He was a big Jimmy Carter supporter and he was telling these right-wingers why they should vote for Carter. And the crazy thing is, he was holding strong even though he was completely outnumbered."

A couple of days later, Dan noticed Michael in the law library and approached him about the hallway commotion he had witnessed. Kolber mentioned that Carter had once been a segregationist and had only recently begun supporting truly progressive principles. "Michael starts getting very serious," Kolber said with a chuckle. "I had to tell him, I'm just messing with you, man."

With that, the two struck up a friendship that was destined to be deep and permanent – a fraternity between two exceptionally intelligent young men, brimming with ideas and not only willing, but eager, to push the envelope, taking on boundaries as sport. With identical class schedules, the two became virtually inseparable on campus, a study in contrasts— Michael, the tall, heavy set, dulcet-toned black man with southern charm; Dan, the slightly built, bespectacled fast-talking Jewish man from Miami with a northeastern edginess. Their professors and fellow students came to understand that, despite their outward differences, Hollis and Kolber were like-minded and team-oriented. When one made a point or argument, the other would back him up or cheer him on. Kolber, who feasted on law books, was always prepared with case law, forensics and his talents as a debater.

Michael and Dan's tag-team antics were not consigned to serious matters. The duo often deployed them in social settings too, like the time they made a trip to Studio 54, the legendary, culture-bending New York City nightclub and favorite celebrity haunt. Despite the well-chronicled naughtiness going on inside the place, the bouncers at Studio 54 were known to be very selective about who was allowed in. Many of the rabble-rousing yet famous got in; many of the proper yet obscure did not.

Full of themselves as always, Michael and Dan cooked up a plan to enhance their chances of admission. On a lark, they decided to exploit a previously noted resemblance between Michael and American diplomat Donald McHenry who was Ambassador Andrew Young's lieutenant at the United Nations. The mischievous duo decided the 17-year age difference between the two men would not be a problem.

"Make way for the ambassador!" Kolber shouted as he and Michael worked their way up the rope line toward the club entrance. "The ambassador needs to get through!"

The mischief worked like a charm and the two colluders quickly found themselves in the midst of a spectacle—blaring music, undulating bodies, dazzling lights, stars like Bianca Jagger and, here and there, trays of powdered cocaine. The scene was everything Michael had heard it would be and he didn't care for it. "He thought it looked like trouble and Michael was not one for trouble," said Kolber. "So, we got outta there."

Despite the rigors and demands of first-year law—make or break time for many a student—Michael maintained his political ties in Atlanta, both because he loved the strategic planning and daring involved and because he wanted to keep his Rolodex current for the sake of his own political future. During a break in classes, he once again helped presidential candidate Jimmy Carter make the rounds in New Hampshire, Michael's old stomping grounds. To Michael's everlasting delight, Carter not only won the New Hampshire primary that February of 1976 and then the Democratic nomination that July, but in November, he defeated sitting President Gerald Ford. Michael was with Carter when victory was declared and one of the first people he called was Dartmouth's John Kemeny, who had helped welcome the then-virtual-unknown to New Hampshire two years earlier. As Jean Kemeny wrote in her book, "A jubilant Mike Hollis called the morning after the election from the Atlanta hotel where President-elect Carter was staying to give John some tips on contacts in the new administration— people to see in the White House. He was bubbling over again with excitement—and very useful information."

That close encounter with big league politics may have lit a fire in his belly because, in his second year of law school, Michael announced to Dan that he had been taking a serious look at the American Bar Association's Law Student Division (L.S.D.), an organization designed to prepare students for the vagaries of professional law. Most of the country's law schools had L.S.D. chapters, where becoming an officer would propel an otherwise ordinary law student into the campus stratosphere. But Michael was not eyeing the leadership of the UVA chapter. He told Dan he wanted the presidency of the 30,000-member national body, one of the largest student professional organizations in the world.

"Until he got it in his head to run the organization," says an amused Dan Kolber, "he hadn't even been a member."

As usual, Kolber leaped into action to help his friend achieve what no other black man or woman had ever accomplished. It was a formidable challenge. The uppermost governing position in the organization was jealously guarded by a good-ole-boys' network and it had one of its own in mind for the presidency. From the start, Michael was viewed, and treated, as an interloper. The reigning powers, all white, presented a united front of opposition, doing all they could to undermine the Hollis candidacy and run him out. But Michael had assembled a cadre of smart and enthusiastic supporters, he worked the membership vigorously, and was so good on his feet, that the diehards had no choice but to concede that they were in for a real fight. Both sides put their last best hopes in on-the-ground efforts at the annual convention that summer of 1977 in Chicago, where the contest would be decided.

For once, Kolber was not with his friend – he was a summer associate at a New York law firm – but he touched bases with Michael several times each day by phone. Another UVA law student, Josh Henson, who would be elected president of the International Law Student Division, helped Michael schmooze the conventioneers. When the votes were tallied, Michael had won the presidency by a single vote.

Not that the puny margin mattered to him. In his mind, a win was a mandate and Michael immediately set out to flex his new political muscle. He fired his rival in the president's race, a man who had expected to resume his job as the student lawyers' chief liaison to the ABA. Michael appointed Kolber to the post, which required frequent travel among the fifteen circuits that constituted the L.S.D. domain. In a bold break with tradition, Michael also directed the national L.S.D. staff to report to him rather than to the ABA. And he persuaded UVA officials to provide him with a deluxe suite of campus offices for the organization's operations, drawing the ire of some faculty members who had been assigned less agreeable accommodations.

Upset by Michael's victory, the old hands in the L.S.D. were feverish about disrupting his term, refusing to cooperate with his directives, accusing him of racism, regularly complaining about him to the ABA, and flooding the association's national offices in Chicago with documents they claimed to be incriminating. "The next thing I know, I am in the middle of this firestorm," Kolber recalled. "I'm getting letters that my reimbursements will not be approved."

But like others before them, Michael's foes had underestimated both his determination and his cunning. He turned on the charm with ABA big wigs and subordinates alike at national headquarters, assuring them that his objective was to transform the L.S.D. from a primarily social organization into a serious-minded training ground for future lawyers. He portrayed the criticisms they'd been hearing as the sour grapes of people who didn't want their joy ride to end.

"There was some push back and there was some embarrassment, but they were no match for Michael," says Kolber, chuckling over the memory. "Imagine him showing up at the ABA offices in Chicago in the Loop. Here, he walks in. They know he's coming. He's got his fan club. He had friends in the ABA."

Michael took on his presidential responsibilities like a turret gunner – focused, intense and panoramic. Directly or through surrogates, he managed every facet of the organization, keeping the ABA abreast of each step he made toward "professionalizing" the division by engaging it in ponderous matters of the day like legal services for the poor, the Bakke case involving alleged "reverse discrimination" in higher education, and lawyer advertising, which was then still in its infancy. He was hopelessly smitten with his girlfriend, Gail Bryant, a student at UVA's medical school, but except for her, little else commanded Michael's time and attention other than running the division. According to Kolber, Michael had never been a devout law student and would wait until exam time to cram a semester's worth of learning into his head. Nor did he seem to care much about grades, though he always got good ones, perhaps because he was known to add a little insurance by earning academic credit for things like helping a professor write a book. Unlike Kolber, Michael was more likely to observe and listen in class rather than engage debate. But, when he did speak up, it was often unforgettable – like the time a professor questioned the clarity of a new Supreme Court decision whose majority opinion was written by the chief justice himself. Kolber recalls the exchange:

Michael: *Regarding the opinion written by Chief Justice Burger, I don't think it's unclear at all.* He then proceeded to explain the ruling.

Professor: *Well, Mr. Hollis, that's very good. But I must warn you that you should never pass your opinion off as fact. That will get you in trouble with a judge someday.*

Michael: *No, that's not my opinion. That is exactly what Chief Justice Burger meant.*

Professor (conspicuously peeved): *How could you possibly be so sure?*

Michael: *Because Chief Justice Burger is a friend of mine, so I called him on the phone and asked him and that's what he told me.*

Michael had gotten to know the most powerful man in the American judiciary by way of his appointment to the Committee to Consider Standards for Admission to Practice in Federal Courts—a group of esteemed judges and law professors chaired by Edward J. Devitt, the highly respected federal judge from Minnesota who pioneered the six-member jury in federal civil trials. Michael was one of only four "student consultants" to the committee, which was an arm of the U.S. Judicial Conference, chaired by Chief Justice Burger.

Even with those rarefied connections—even with his presidency well underway—Michael was constantly hounded by adversaries determined to punish him for alleged or imagined offenses—so much so that, near the end of his term, they moved to impeach him as L.S.D. president. Michael responded with a lengthy letter accusing his critics of a politically motivated vendetta against him. Privately, Michael let Kolber know that he was concerned about the group's continuing harassment, particularly the impeachment threat.

"He said, 'What are we going to do?' I said, 'You graduate. By the time they go through this process, you're out. You're done. You've run the clock on them.'" And that's what they did. Michael earned his Juris doctorate degree from UVA in May 1978 with only a few months remaining in his term as L.S.D. president—summer months, when little serious business got done.

If the student lawyers expected a timorous Michael Hollis at their annual convention in Chicago that August, they were in for a surprise. Even though he was the lame duck president, Michael arrived to preside over the convention seemingly as confident and swaggering as ever, catered to by an entourage of staff and supporters. He even brought along a gift of sorts for the delegates: a free, twelve-page magazine called *The New Lawyer* with a full-page photo of Michael and the chief justice of the United States shaking hands and smiling like old friends as its cover.

Michael had published the magazine on his own, filling it with reprints of columns he had written for *The Student Lawyer*, the Law Student Division's official monthly publication. Chief Justice Burger was in town to address the ABA and his keynote address was to include a mention of one of Michael's columns about restructuring law school studies, a proposition the chief justice would commend to the bar. When the editor of *The Student Lawyer* got wind of Justice Burger's intentions, he informed the ABA brass about Michael's rogue publication. In turn, ABA officials cautioned Justice Burger that the article he wanted to reference, though written by Michael, had first appeared in a different publication and that neither Michael's reprinting of it nor his composite magazine had the organization's approval. In his speech, the chief justice commended Michael's argument about law school reform, but sidestepped the controversy by noting that his position had been proffered in two publications.

Still hell-bent on some kind of disciplinary action, Michael's detractors engineered a vote of reprimand against their outgoing president. More than two-thirds of the delegates approved the measure, but it had no practical effect other than to win the notice of *The National Law Journal*, the legal world's preeminent publication. The *Journal* reported the "Convention Brouhaha" the next month, replete with a photograph of that *New Lawyer* cover—the one with Michael and Chief Justice Burger cheerily greeting one another. The article also noted that Michael had asked the ABA to reimburse him around $1,500 for his magazine's production costs, another example of the Hollis moxie.

Bitterness from that contentious year outlived Michael's tenure. In 1981, an assistant district attorney in Suffolk County, Massachusetts, sent a letter to Dartmouth's Board of Trustees, challenging Michael's nomination to the board. Sharon D. Meyers, who had been active in UVA's Law Student

Division chapter, charged that Michael's presidency had been riddled with racism, malfeasance, incompetence, and investigations. Michael pounced.

"I have never received any reprimand from anybody, including the ABA, or the Law Student Division," Michael wrote in a letter to the Dartmouth Board in early April 1981. But, what about that vote to reprimand him at the 1978 convention? "Pursuant to ABA procedures, any such reprimand could only result from a hearing affording me due process. No such hearing was ever held," Michael's letter argued. "I have never misused funds, abused authority or made misrepresentations of fact to any governing body. Ms. Meyers' allegations to the contrary are libelous per se."

The letter painted a picture of the atmosphere surrounding his presidency of L.S.D. and portrayed Meyers as a disgruntled member with a score to settle.

"Ms. Meyers (who is not a Dartmouth alumnae) was one of the individuals who was a part of the prior administration, whose candidate, programs and policies I defeated and repudiated," it said. "From the beginning, this faction attempted to subvert the will of the majority and engage in political attacks against me and my administration."

The day after writing that letter, Michael called Meyers' boss to complain that she had used official letterhead for her antagonistic letter to the Dartmouth trustees—a violation of state law, which prohibits the use of public property and resources for personal purposes. Accordingly, First Assistant District Attorney Paul K. Leary shortly wrote a letter to Dartmouth, confirming that his office "did not sanction the use of its official letterhead in a letter sent by Ms. Meyers dated March 26, 1981. The contents of the letter are a personal statement by Ms. Meyers and do not in any way reflect the opinion or belief of the District Attorney."

Even though Michael had discredited his critic, the spitefulness of Meyers' accusations and the aspersions cast upon his character and reputation sickened him. But he was in no mood for re-fighting old battles over ground he had long since vacated and he resented the attempts to undo him after so much time. Meyers' dirty work could shroud his seat on the board in suspicion and awkwardness and he loved his alma mater too much to invite such trouble, even if it was not of his making. He had been a faithful and loyal alum, steering many a promising high school graduate toward Dartmouth and facilitating their admittance—his adored niece, Julius and Jeanne's daughter, Christiana; family friend Ty Moddelmog, the son of the CEO of the Metro Atlanta Chamber of Commerce; and James Bernard's nephew by marriage, Rembert Browne, who would go on to become a respected writer for *New York Magazine* all matriculated at Dartmouth with Michael's help. As much as he wanted to top off his Dartmouth experience with a board membership, Michael would not allow controversy to besmirch his proud record. Regretfully, he withdrew his name from consideration as a candidate for Dartmouth's board.

Virginia Robinson Hollis taught her children to work hard, dream big and prepare themselves for opportunity.

Michael Robinson Hollis at Age 2.

Michael grew up in the shadow of historic Morehouse College.

For decades, the Butler Street YMCA was the nerve center of Atlanta's black leadership.

Dr. Benjamin Mays (left), the esteemed president of Morehouse, was one of Michael's most revered mentors and surrogate fathers. Prominent dentist Dr. Harvey Smith (right) was another such father figure and helped young Michael in his cake-selling business.

John Cox, executive director of the Butler YMCA, was politically astute and connected. He helped kindle Michael's interest in civic life.

Michael was inspired by his serendipitous encounter with Dr. Martin Luther King, Jr., the unexpected officiant at cousin Thelma McClenton's 1964 wedding at historic Ebenezer Baptist Church.

Virginia Hollis and Leila Williams forged a close friendship when both worked at The Busy Bee, which was a popular haunt of Atlanta's black civic and business leaders.

Michael as a teenager, circa 1969.

Michael was a proud and accomplished graduate of Booker T. Washington High, Atlanta's first public high school for African-Americans.

Virginia Hollis always encouraged her children to stand on principle and to be involved in civic affairs.

James Bernard Arnold, Michael's older half-brother, on graduation day at Atlanta University, 1968.

Michael's sister, Ruth, was only one
year older, but doted on her brother.

Happy siblings (from left) Flem, Jr.,
Virginia Elaine and Michael Hollis.

Michael with Joan Hollis Mitchell, his half-sister
(left), and James Bernard's wife, Pat Arnold.

Michael holding his niece, Christina,
with his beloved mother and brother,
Julius (Christina's father) by his side.

Mrs. Hollis (seated, center) at Decatur
Seventh Day Adventist Church, where she
was a respected church elder.

Michael surprised many by deciding to attend
Dartmouth College in Hanover, NH.

Michael, an unknown fellow Dartmouth student, and Atlanta's Julian Bond, then a Georgia state representative.

Michael, in a speech at Dartmouth. He was so business-like and precocious that fellow students nicknamed him "the governor."

Michael at Dartmouth.

President Jimmy Carter greets Michael at the White House. It was Michael who had made sure the once-little-known Georgia governor met key New Hampshire politicos before running for president in 1976.

(From left) Michael's friend, collaborator and fellow UVA law student Dan Kolber; William Spann, president of the American Bar Assn.; Michael; and Frank Hereford, UVA president.

Law student Michael Hollis addressing a Meeting of the American Bar Association's Law Student Division. Michael was president.

As associate legal counsel for the President's Commission on the Accident at Three Mile Island, Michael briefs the commission chairman, his old friend and mentor, Dartmouth President John Kemeny.

Michael is recognized by Atlanta Mayor Maynard Jackson at City Hall. Jackson took on both the black and white establishment in becoming the first African-American mayor of a major American city.

Michael's devotion to and adoration of his mother was one of his hallmarks, known to all.

CHAPTER 6

It had to be heady stuff to return to his hometown with an undergraduate degree from the Ivy League, a law degree from the university founded by Thomas Jefferson, a national profile by virtue of his presidency of the ABA's Law Student Division, and a friendship with the president of the United States and then get hired by Atlanta's largest and most prominent law firm. Still, it wasn't long before Michael was ready to move on from his position as an associate at Hansell Post Brandon & Dorsey. The experience rendered several potentially valuable new contacts and would mean a star on his resume for having worked for one of the South's most prestigious white-shoe firms. His concentration on land lease-back transactions had also taught him about the intricacies of high finance and he was eager to test what he had learned. But more than anything, the Hansell Post job taught him that he was not cut out for practicing law. It was simply too mundane and predictable for someone like him.

An escape hatch opened seven months after Michael went to work for Hansell Post. The meltdown at the Three Mile Island nuclear generating plant near Harrisburg, Pennsylvania in late March 1979, had alarmed the nation about nuclear energy generally and radioactive fallout from the accident particularly and President Carter wanted answers. Two weeks after the accident, the president signed an executive order establishing a twelve-member investigative commission with none other than Dartmouth's John Kemeny as chairman. Thanks to his connections to Kemeny, Michael was one of three young attorneys hired to assist the commission's five senior lawyers in taking depositions, gathering documents and interviewing experts. Although the work was tedious and involved a lot of travel, Michael relished his new authority, especially when big shots responded to him with condescension or dismissiveness, as did an executive at Metropolitan Edison, one of the three companies that owned the damaged nuclear power plant. When the man tried to bluff his way out of the deposition, Michael coolly advised him that he could submit voluntarily or by force of the federal government. Thus did the utility giant pooh-bah surrender to the rookie lawyer with subpoena power.

In addition to boosting his ego and putting him on the front lines of a major current event, the job meant frequent trips to Washington, D.C., where he would drop in on the Carter administration's large cast of Georgians, some of whom he had known most of his life, some he had worked with in the presidential campaign, and others he had only met after Carter took the White House. The Carter people were already gearing up for the 1980 re-election campaign and sweating out a potential primary challenge from Senator Ted Kennedy, who was dominating the early popularity polls.

Michael's sojourns to Washington also allowed him to spend more time with Julius, who remained in the nation's capital after Congressman Young departed for the United Nations as U.S. ambassador. Julius was working at the Export-Import Bank, putting together deals to facilitate foreign purchases of U.S. goods in service to the balance of trade. Julius made a point of widening his younger brother's circle of friends by introducing him to government veterans and political operatives who knew the ins-and-outs of federal affairs—people who could make things happen.

The President's Commission on the Accident at Three Mile Island concluded its work in October 1979. In early December, President Carter announced measures for implementing the commission's recommendations and thanked Kemeny, et al, for their service. Even after the commission disbanded, Michael continued darting between Atlanta and Washington, dabbling in the Carter campaign, building his network of friends and associates and imagining a political career of his own. When he was home in Atlanta, he spent many of his waking hours at City Hall, most often in the mayor's office where Maynard Jackson was continuing to change the complexion of Atlanta politics while dodging bullets of consternation from white business leaders counting the days until the end of the mayor's second four-year term—by law, the limit for tenure. More than a year earlier, Michael had delivered a 15-page memorandum to Mayor Jackson, urging him to seek the presidency in 1980 and laying out a strategy for victory. Dan Kolber, who helped Michael write the memo, said it was inspired by British-born physician and liberal activist Peter Bourne's famous thesis arguing for a Carter candidacy in 1976.

Michael had been a friend and helpmate to Jimmy Carter in the president's first White House campaign, but he would have relished a Jackson candidacy. After all, Maynard Jackson was his idol, every bit the fearless and shrewd avatar of self-determination that Michael considered himself to be. Add to that their friendship and their Atlanta kinship and Maynard was practically family.

The fact was, when it came to politics, Michael was first and foremost a pragmatist with black empowerment at the top of his agenda. That focus explains Michael's long fascination with Richard Nixon, one of the most tortured personalities to ever take the Oval Office. Before Nixon's sickeningly racist sentiments toward blacks and Jews came to light – and before his culpability a la Watergate was exposed – Michael had admired the 38th president for his support of black capitalism. It was Nixon, after all, who set quotas and timetables for minority participation in federal contracts. And he was the president who, by executive order, created the Office of Minority Business Enterprise, assisting black- and woman-owned businesses in gaining access to much-needed capital and previously unavailable markets. Unlike soul singer James Brown, Michael did not give his vote to Nixon in 1972, but he agreed with the way the showman saw the president's obligation to black people, as captured in Brown's lyric: "I don't want nobody giving me nothing. Open up the door; I'll get it myself."

Although the memo to Mayor Jackson was the product of young, eager and somewhat naïve enthusiasts, it was comprehensive, well-researched and full of blandishments. Michael and Jackson talked it over, but ultimately the mayor resisted his young friend's enticement and chose to complete his second term as mayor. Michael remained in the Carter camp. However disappointed either man may have been initially, both eventually had to have been glad they stayed put. That year, Carter vanquished the Kennedy challenge, beating the senator by more than two-to-one in the primaries, only to be annihilated by Republican Ronald Reagan in the November general election. Jackson's decision almost assuredly spared him a demoralizing career setback and a lot of squandered real and political capital. Michael too, to a lesser degree.

"I recall Maynard telling the rest of us on his team about Michael," said Shirley Franklin, the city's Commissioner for Cultural Affairs who would later become Atlanta's first woman mayor. "Maynard was clearly a fan of Michael's. He was a bold, innovative thinker and so was Michael. And Maynard was completely fascinated by Michael's business acumen."

Jackson's oldest child, Brooke, recalls her father's fondness for Michael.

"Daddy was very impressed with Michael," she said. "He said he was this young, dynamic lawyer who's got a great education and has accomplished a lot." More than a decade later, when she and her father would form Jackmont Hospitality, their lucrative food service management company, "Michael was an endless source of good advice on how to pull together initial financing – where was the best source of financing, the most reliable source of capital, and how to approach them," Brooke Jackson says.

In some instances, Michael made the introductions between Brooke and prospective financiers.

Michael maintained a small law office in Atlanta while he contemplated his next move. His interest in public finance and investment banking had not waned just because he was no longer working on land lease-back and municipal finance transactions for Hansell Post. Feeling a tug from the country's financial nerve center, Michael got himself hired by Oppenheimer and Company, a top investment banking firm on Wall Street. Even though he had not a whit of professional experience in the fast-paced, high-stakes investment world, Michael insisted on an executive position. On Day One, he arrived at Oppenheimer as vice president of public finance. The job often had him on the road marketing municipal bond underwriting services, but not so much that he couldn't enjoy one of the world's most dynamic cities and all it had to offer a young, single, professional man in the 1980s.

Living in New York reunited Michael with two close, old friends: Gary Love, his fellow Dartmouth alum, and Kolber, his trusted collaborator from law school. Already in investment banking, Love worked for a different firm on a different floor of the same office tower as Michael and the two even lived in the same apartment building on the Upper East Side of Manhattan. When they weren't entertaining clients, traveling, or carousing in one of the city's countless bars or restaurants, they might be found together on any given night or weekend cooking, drinking, and shooting the breeze about things past, present and future as Smokey Robinson's smooth falsetto oozed from the stereo. Love remembers that Michael was champing at the bit to convert what he was learning at Oppenheimer into a business—or two or more—of his own. "I know his plan was not to stay [in investment banking] for long," says Love. "He just needed to learn enough to be able to raise capital and be fluent in business terms."

Kolber was now married to Lesley, the woman he had fallen in love with when he was studying law and she was in nursing school at the University of Virginia. Although he and his best friend were once again in the same town, the demands of married life and work as an associate at a large international law firm left Kolber little time for socializing. He still had to rely mostly on telephone calls to keep in touch with Michael.

Sometimes, the calls would go on for hours with the two old friends talking shop, politics, and personal matters. Many of them also devolved into what Kolber describes as "bullshit" sessions, with him and Michael volleying business ideas between themselves, looking for ways to break out of the rat race that left each man feeling exhausted and unfulfilled. The popular lore is that Michael got the idea of starting an airline from a colleague at Oppenheimer, but Kolber says it was during one of their brainstorming sessions that the concept for Air Atlanta took shape. Kolber recalls that Michael had been developing the idea since 1979, not long after a momentous change took place in the commercial airline industry.

Until the Deregulation Act of 1978, the U.S. Civil Aeronautics Board (C.A.B.) exercised stingy control over airline routes and rates. Proposed new airlines had to go through a convoluted and tedious process that could take years to exhaust. It took a protracted C.A.B. review for an established airline to add even one route per year. The result was limited competition, limited destinations and fare levels so high that flying was out of the question as a routine means of travel for many people of ordinary means. C.A.B.-approved rates built in a "reasonable" profit for the airlines on each ticket.

The entire industry, from CEOs to baggage workers, opposed deregulation. But Democrats on Capitol Hill, led by Senator Kennedy, favored deregulation in the name of consumer rights. Republicans on the Hill wanted it for the sake of free market competition. The chairman of the C.A.B., economist Alfred Kahn, was one of the measure's staunchest proponents and the president respected his views especially; Kahn had been Carter's chief economic adviser. Kahn's advocacy and the bipartisan nature of support made way for Carter to sign the bill in October 1978.

Now that they no longer had to prove there was a public need for their services—the old qualifier—airline startups began flooding in, eager to demonstrate the new standard: that they were fit, willing and able to provide commercial passenger or cargo services.

To Michael, the new opportunity seemed tailor-made for him. He was itching to start his own business and this one required the kind of gutsiness he had in spades and for which he was already noted. It also was in line with his hometown's signature enterprise, commercial aviation. Plus, he had friends in high places to help it happen – the mayor of one of the country's busiest airport cities, for one; his friends on Wall Street for another; and, by good fortune, a member of the C.A.B. itself.

Julius just happened to be leasing his Vermont Avenue condominium from George Dalley, a former congressional aide and State Department official whom Carter appointed to the C.A.B., making Dalley its first black member. The two became fast friends, dining together once a week to catch up on happenings in the nation's bustling capital. As he was wont to do, Julius made sure that Michael and George Dalley knew one another.

"I'm sitting in my office at the Export-Import Bank, Michael comes into my office, closes the door and says, 'Look man, I'm going to run something past you,'" Julius recalls. "He said, 'I've done my research and with the deregulation of the airlines and C.A.B., I'm going to put an airline together.'" Michael told his brother he was going to resign from Oppenheimer and "put all my energy into this."

Julius was speechless. He knew his brother was brilliant, ambitious, brimming with self-confidence, and an entrepreneur to his core. But a 27-year-old black man owning a commercial passenger airline? He leaned back in his chair and stared at Michael in long silence. Finally, Julius pulled out a pen and a notepad. "Ok. What's the plan?" he asked.

For nearly two hours, the Hollis brothers poured over the details about the kind of airline Michael envisioned; where he would get the planes, the pilots, the mechanics; what it would take to get certification; and how much money they would need. Even with home turf advantage, starting the new airline was going to require herculean efforts; that was for sure. But the Hollis boys thrived on big challenges. They were electrified by contests of wit and will. They didn't waste time on the impossible, but the improbable excited them.

Things moved quickly after that. Julius began planning his own moves. With a Republican administration on its way to Washington, it was only a matter of time – and not much of it – before he and other Democratic operatives would need to move on anyway. Now, he had a mission. He would leave the Ex-Im bank sooner rather than later and move back to Atlanta to help smooth the way for Michael's grand proposition. For starters, he could help get Andy Young elected mayor in 1981 and "play the inside game" to make sure that Young – Maynard Jackson's handpicked successor – was on board.

"Michael had extensive conversations with Maynard, who did a lot to move the ball forward," Julius said. "We had to make sure that the enthusiasm carried over into the Young administration."

Just before Christmas 1980, Michael wrote a "memorandum for the files" that he shared with Julius and Kolber, outlining the first steps in getting his airline off the ground.

"If we can come up with the required seed money, I am confident that we can raise the $30-50 million needed to commence operations as a Southwest-type airline out of Midfield," read the memo. He noted that the C.A.B. "wants to encourage competition, and looks favorably toward short haul/low fare carriers" like his envisioned airline. The memo anticipated a public stock offering in six to eight months priced at seven to eleven dollars per share.

"The timing is excellent for this project," Michael continued in the memo. "Our friends in the city will help us with gate access and maintenance, etc. Moreover, my friends on Wall Street are very excited about the prospects, and have already shown a willingness to assist in our efforts."

Despite his abiding optimism, Michael was not foolhardy. With no experience in commercial aviation, he knew better than to rely on his own excitement and fancying for such a large-scale and expensive undertaking.

"Michael was only 27, didn't have $500 of his own and had absolutely zero airline experience," Kolber says. "But by that time, I knew Hollis well and what he was capable of. If he said he would start an airline, then you could bet he would start an airline."

Neither youth, the absence of experience nor adverse odds had ever deterred Michael when he got an idea in his head – not when he went into the cake-selling business as a 10-year-old, not when he talked his way into a job with the Atlanta Braves as a teenager, not when he broke into the American Bar Association's Law Student Division and took it over. To him, age was irrelevant if you knew your stuff and Michael had the regulatory requirements, market picture, and financial requisites down pat. It was undeniable that he did not know the intricacies of running an airline, but he understood that there was no paucity of people who did and that the expertise of most, if not all, could be had for a price. His chief role and challenge would be raising the tens of millions it would take to get the wheels turning. But, he had always been superb at making a case and win-ning people's confidence. All he needed to know was where the money was and who controlled the purse strings.

"This objective will require that I put together a first-rate team to do the feasibility and legal work necessary to raise the larger monies needed to commence operations," Michael wrote in the December memo. "The leading airline consultant firm … has agreed to do the feasibility study and assist in all aspects of the start-up venture." He had also met with top legal specialists in aviation law, describing them as "excited about the prospects."

In early March 1981, Simat Helliesen & Eichner, arguably the coun-try's preeminent aviation consulting firm, delivered to Michael its prelimi-nary analysis of "an Atlanta-based short haul specialist carrier." It presented the venture as a daunting one, but as long as the firm considered it do-able, Michael was encouraged. A high degree of difficulty was no deal-breaker.

"Ok, we will have our work cut out for us," Michael scribbled in a note to his compatriots. "This study is very preliminary but gives an indi-cation of the opportunity. Keep your fingers crossed!!"

The new airline did not have even a name at that point, but it was already gaining speed for takeoff.

CHAPTER 7

When the rest of the family learned of Michael's grand intentions, their reaction was not unlike Julius'—speechless at first, then excited by the possibilities and willing to pitch in however they could.

"When he said he was going to start an airline, we said, 'Go for it,'" recalls his sister, Virginia Elaine. "I knew if he said he was going to do it, it was going to be done. And it was going to be top quality."

Virginia Hollis and Leila Williams backed their pride and praises with money. Both women had worked hard, lived modestly and saved wisely, but it was still a surprise to Michael that his mother and godmother had managed to salt away nearly $35,000 between them and were willing to part with every dime of it to jump start his dream. There wasn't any second-guessing about the decision on their part. They knew that Michael was not one for making empty promises. He was not given to fantasy or pie-in-the-sky. He was not one of the many who dreamed big but had no follow-through—"all talk and no hat," as they say in the South. One way or another, the ladies knew, he'd make good on their faithful investment.

"That was the heaven-blessed seed money that he used to attract the first serious investment," Julius recalls. "So, we couldn't fail because that would be risking the life savings of the two most important women in our lives—our mother and godmother."

With the women's contribution and what he and Julius could pull together, Michael proceeded with the preliminaries of putting together an airline. He had been paying close attention to another post-deregulation startup that was making waves in the industry and decided to model his approach after it.

People Express made its maiden flight on the last day of April 1981 when a mostly empty, used Boeing 737-100 took off for Buffalo, New York, from Terminal C at Newark International, an off-the-beaten-path airport sorely in need of repairs and upgrades. The few passengers on board had paid $23 each for the trip, less than what it would have cost them to drive the 400 miles and without the wear and tear. Word about the new, cut-rate airline spread quickly and, within weeks of the maiden voyage, nearly every People Express flight was sold out. Demand grew so fast that the startup quickly added more planes and destinations along the East coast. By the end of its first year of operations, People Express had transported nearly one million passengers, many of them first-time flyers.

The concept was not entirely new. The father of the "no frills" airline was an Englishman named Freddie Laker, who launched Laker Airways in 1966. In the U.S., Southwest Airlines had long reigned as king of the frill-free model, offering cheap fares, peanuts in lieu of meals, and open instead of assigned seating. But People Express founder Donald Burr, a former cohort of Texas airline magnate Frank Lorenzo, had taken the approach to a new level. In addition to drastically cutting passenger fares, Burr's startup also cut out free baggage checks and free inflight beverages, making it the first to unbundle services so that passengers would have to choose and pay a la carte for what had been standard inclusions. Checking a bag would cost the People Express passenger an extra three dollars; a soft drink could be purchased for fifty cents.

There were other innovations on the operations side – most notably, Burr's labor scheme. He required his non-union employees to pitch in on jobs other than those suggested by their titles, meaning that someone hired as a ticket agent might also sometimes serve as a flight attendant and vice versa. Burr maintained that this "cross-utilization" enhanced efficiency and productivity and fostered unity by forcing employees to walk in each other's shoes. He also required his workers to buy shares of stock in the airline – at discounted prices – so they would have a proprietary interest in the company's reputation and progress. Too, People's pilots and flight attendants were paid considerably less than their peers at established airlines and, uniquely, all employees were salaried, not hourly wage-earners.

People Express had been in the skies for two weeks when Air Atlanta was incorporated in the State of Delaware in May 1981 with 27-year-old Michael Hollis as the new company's chief executive officer and chairman of its one-member board of directors. A few days after incorporation, the board doubled in size with the election of Robert J. White, the president of the National Alliance of Postal and Federal Employees (NAPFE).

NAPFE had been around since 1913, when black railway mail clerks from across the country came together in Chattanooga, Tennessee to form an industrial and benevolent group to protect their job security and economic interests. The vast majority of railway mail clerks were black when the railroads used wooden cars to transport letters and parcels for the Post Office. The cars and their paper contents were usually positioned behind the locomotives, making them especially susceptible to catching fire from the big engines or the oil lamps used for lighting. Clerks also had to deal with a high risk of derailment and with hold-ups that were so frequent and frightening that the federal government ordered clerks to carry guns. Because of those dangers, white workers shunned the assignment, hence the prevalence of black men in the mail cars.

Once the railroads began replacing wooden cars with safer and more expensive steel cars, the jobs became more attractive to whites, many of whom were keen on President Woodrow Wilson's new racial segregation policy for the federal workforce, which was ardently enforced by U.S. Postmaster General Albert Burleson. Black clerks were shut out from membership in the white clerk's union, the Railway Mail Association. Left to fend for themselves, African-American clerks formed NAPFE, whose membership was eventually opened to all federal workers.

It is believed that Atlanta's own John Wesley Dobbs was one of the men who traveled to Chattanooga that hot August day in 1913 when

NAPFE was established. It would make sense that he was there since he was one of the most respected railway mail clerks at the time and was rising in the ranks when most black clerks were stuck for years in their original jobs. At any rate, he was a charter member and an active one throughout his thirty-two-year career on the railroad.

As Dobbs' grandson, Maynard Jackson was well versed in NAPFE's history. He knew that the organization had maintained its commitment to social justice and was aware that the commitment extended to its investments. For example, in 1977, NAPFE had moved $250,000 of its treasure from old line banks to five minority lending institutions as a show of support for President Carter's appeal for federal agencies to do business with black banks. It only made sense to Jackson that his late grandfather's organization would be interested in a man who was defying the odds and laying the foundation for an enterprise unprecedented in the annals of black business.

As a young teenager working after school at Leila Williams' restaurant, Michael had impressed the president of the local NAPFE chapter, Charles Harper, with his personality, work ethic and intelligence. Now, years later, upon Maynard Jackson's entreaty, Harper was willing to support Michael's business proposition and recommend that NAPFE help back it. Harper and Jackson's ringing endorsements, coupled with Michael's unerring presentation, made a believer out of NAPFE's national president, Robert White, who was optimistic that his organization would help fund the new airline. Not all of his NAPFE colleagues were on board, however.

Some were nervous about the gamble. After all, for years, NAPFE had been so risk-averse that it kept its money in a simple interest-bearing savings account.

Fortunately for Michael, White was persistent and it helped that the former mayor of Atlanta had given his full backing. It was likewise significant that Michael was willing to put up about $100,000 of his own, given that he and Julius had pooled their money with the contributions from their mother and Leila Williams. After weeks of back-and-forth, White ultimately prevailed and the organization's investment arm wrote a check for $500,000 to Air Atlanta, hedged by 400,000 shares of stock.

More than half a million dollars was an encouraging start, but it was a far cry from the tens of millions needed to launch an airline. Nonetheless, it would prove to potential investors that Michael was serious about his airline proposal and would also go a long way toward the costs of satisfying the Civil Aeronautics Board's exacting requirements. Michael had hired some of the country's top economic analysts, lawyers and financial consultants to handle the C.A.B. application so that he could concentrate on fund-raising and wooing veteran executives to his nascent airline.

Although he had Julius and Maynard Jackson to call upon, Michael's chief collaborator and "ace boon coon," Dan Kolber was still in New York, nine hundred miles away. Michael constantly appealed to him to move to Atlanta so they could work together more conveniently. But Dan and Lesley had just had their first child that summer of 1981, and he needed more assurance that the airline would get off the ground before he and his wife quit their jobs and uprooted the young family. When he could, Kolber would parachute into Atlanta for critical meetings, but he and Michael tackled their endless To-Do list mostly by telephone, discussing the availability of air-worthy planes, making sure they had a handle on all of the regulatory and bureaucratic hoops, laying the political groundwork in Atlanta, and more than anything else, figuring out how to finance their ambitious undertaking.

"From 1981 on, I probably spoke to Mike every night during the week about Air Atlanta," Kolber recalls. "I would get home around 8 p.m. and then he and I would talk until well after midnight."

Michael scored his first hiring victory when Roden A. Brandt joined Air Atlanta as president and CEO in November 1981. Brandt had been lured from Pan Am, where he had been senior vice president for airline planning. He had been an executive with National Airlines and Eastern Airlines before that. The terms of his two-year Air Atlanta contract included a $75,000 annual salary, a $25,000 bonus upon approval of the C.A.B. application, and another $25,000 bonus in his second year of employment. Pension, profit-sharing and stock option plans complemented customary employee benefits like health and life insurance policies and paid vacations. One month later, Michael and Robert White voted to add Brandt to the board of directors, along with Robin H.H. Wilson, the president of the Long Island Railroad and a former senior vice president at TransWorld Airlines. Then, on January 1, 1982, James E. Purcell, a longtime official with the Federal Aviation Administration, came on board as vice president of operations. The hiring of two seasoned aviation professionals and the election of a transportation mogul to the board bolstered the airline's credibility, enhancing the likelihood of major investments and C.A.B. approval.

Jackson continued to work with Mayor Young to ensure that the magnificent new airport terminal he had helped build would be accommodating to Air Atlanta once it was wheels up. He was no longer mayor, but eight high-profile years in office had put him in touch with many of the wealthiest people in the country, most of them in the state, and all of them in the city. He knew where the money was and advised Michael on when and how to broach the issue, making introductions as needed.

As a history-making mayor of a major American city, Jackson, only 43 years old, was a hot commodity in the legal and business world. But he was determined to remain in Atlanta, the city he loved and helped build, and therein lay the rub.

The white business establishment was still nursing its old, hard grudge over having been forced to share lucrative city contracts, particularly those related to the expansion of Hartsfield International Airport. Delta's top men, CEO David Garrett, Jr., and COO Ronald W. Allen, had been infuriated by Jackson's minority contracting and joint venture directives in the airport expansion project. They had released an arsenal against Jackson to thwart his plan for black empowerment, but Jackson had outmaneuvered them at every turn.

With Jackson out of office, the Good Ole Boy Network seemed to think it could reclaim access to and influence over the second floor at City

Hall as the last laugh at its nemesis. Moreover, now that Jackson needed a job, disgruntled white business leaders had another opportunity to exact revenge: they could blackball him. The former mayor had every qualification almost any business could ask for – great education, redoubtable executive experience, an astute and inventive mind, youthful vigor and contacts galore – yet not one law firm or financial institution in Atlanta would hire the man they blamed for spoiling their banquet.

Michael felt obligated to help and solicited Kolber's assistance in finding an appropriate landing spot for their old friend. Notwithstanding Jackson's resolve to stay in Atlanta, they knew they would have to look outside the city to find companies that were both prestigious enough for the former mayor and respectful of his value. They arranged a meeting with Bob Traurig of Miami, a close family friend of Kolber and partner in what would later become the third largest law firm in the United States. The firm offered a position to Jackson, but since Greenberg Traurig LLP was strictly a Florida firm at the time, Jackson declined the offer. Fortunately, another prominent law firm, Chicago-based Chapman Cutler, was willing to hire Jackson and set up an Atlanta office whence he became the rainmaker everyone knew he could be.

On March 8, 1982, Air Atlanta filed its formal application with the Civil Aeronautics Board in Washington. It was a thick digest of the What's, How's, and When's of "the first prospective new entrant proposing high frequency, low-fare passenger service from Atlanta's Hartsfield International

Airport." Its substantial batch of exhibits and attachments included testimonials from Michael, Brandt, and Purcell. While others focused mainly on their credentials and projections for the new airline, Michael's testimony read more like a mission statement, emphasizing the airline's purposefulness as an instrument of public service and a tool of democracy.

"Others may differ, but in my opinion, nothing has influenced the advancement of civilization and social change greater than development and expansion of modes of transportation," the statement said. "Our Founding Fathers knew that the right of mobility and travel from state to state was such a great equalizer among men that they protected that right in the Constitution.

"Historically, because of the high cost of air travel, the safest, most efficient and comfortable means of transportation has been denied to many Americans—until now; until the advent of the regional, specialized low-cost carriers. Our objective is to make Air Atlanta, Inc., a common carrier in the truest sense of that phrase. The technology is available, competent and knowledgeable personnel are willing, capital will rise to its optimum level of use, and our projections show thousands of potential airline passengers are waiting to leave their cars and buses and fly Air Atlanta, Inc." It was a seductive blend of pragmatism and idealism, speaking to both the measurable benefits and moral advantages of Air Atlanta's commencement.

The application proposed to start operations in the summer of 1982 with four aircraft making four daily flights from Atlanta Hartsfield to Raleigh-Durham, North Carolina; five daily flights to Memphis and

Nashville, Tennessee; and six to Tampa, Florida. It anticipated adding four more markets and four additional aircraft within a year and a half.

The airline would have a two-tier fare structure, a la the Southwest Airlines innovation. A one-way, nonstop coach ticket would be priced at 45 percent or more below the going rate during peak travel hours; 50 percent or more below the other airlines' rates for off-peak flights. For example, where existing airlines charged $104 for a nonstop coach flight from Atlanta to Memphis during the heaviest travel times of the day, Air Atlanta would charge $59 for the same trip. The application predicted that Air Atlanta's load factor—the percentage of paid seats—would reach the break-even point of 51.5 percent by the end of its first full year of operations.

At the same time that it filed the application, Air Atlanta submitted a motion for expedited treatment, urging the C.A.B. to approve the application by the middle of April, which would have been a seven-week turnaround. It argued that a fast track decision would allow the airline to "promote a private placement of its securities in time for a summer 1982 start-up"—in other words, a public offering to raise capital.

"Issuance of a certificate to Air Atlanta pursuant to expedited procedures will ensure that it will be in a position to seek and obtain financing in time for start-up in summer 1982 if market conditions permit," read the airline's motion for expedited treatment. "It will also allow Southeastern consumers the first real choice in low fares and frequency and service options, which the Congress sought to create in enacting the Airline Deregulation

Act, and further reduce public dependence upon the private automobile for business and recreational travel."

It was not a gratuitous argument, given that Delta's domination at Hartsfield International had allowed it to flex its considerable political muscle and minimize the competition at its main hub, resulting in a 19 percent premium on its flights out of Atlanta. But, the prospect of a public offering was at the real force behind the argument for speeding up certification. Air Atlanta's till was quickly being depleted by preparatory expenses, Brandt and Purcell's salaries and benefits, and other early outlays. If he was going to replenish it, Michael needed hard evidence that his proposition was not just wishful thinking but had measurable momentum. He understood that major investors would not take a gamble on a good idea alone, not even one as well-developed and diligently researched as his. He needed an official Certificate of Public Convenience and Necessity from the C.A.B. and he needed it stat.

At the end of May, an administrative law judge ruled Air Atlanta fit to fly. Two weeks later, the C.A.B. waived its right to review the ruling and approved the application, issuing the coveted certificate on June 15, 1982. The process had taken two months.

A few days after certification was granted, during a capital-raising swing throughout the northeast corridor, Michael, Brandt, and Maynard Jackson stopped by the White House at the invitation of Vice President George H. W. Bush who wanted to congratulate his guests on their new certification. Bush praised Air Atlanta as a harbinger of good jobs and better days in Atlanta and volunteered his help with the Federal Aviation Administration in the event Air Atlanta ran into any problems obtaining landing slots at Hartsfield. In his ensuing talks with potential financiers, Michael always made a point of mentioning the vice president's recognition and offer.

While making the rounds on Wall Street, Michael received some startling news from an investment banker friend at the Dillon Read brokerage firm. According to the banker, investors' zeal for the People Express model had run its course and was beginning to wane. Although the airline had broken the mold and was still creating a sensation, some thought it was growing too fast, outpacing Donald Burr's mom-and-pop labor model, and flirting with disaster by taking the major carriers on head-to-head, even at their own hubs. The big money was no longer inclined toward low-rate startups.

The news took the wind out of Kolber's sails. All of their work had been modeled after People Express. It was the prototype embedded in the C.A.B. application, the premise of its newly won certification. Now, they were back to square one.

Prone to idealism, Kolber had been looking forward to developing an airline that would serve two purposes dear to his heart: making money and serving the public interest—the old "doing well while doing good" creed. He implored his good friend to stay the course and stick with the original plan to make Air Atlanta an affordable conveyance for ordinary folks, but Michael had already begun researching alternatives. It was one of the few times that the two men had divergent views but, as Kolber learned, his insistence was pointless. Michael had changed his mind and closed it down. He wasted no time in commissioning a new business plan to show prospective investors. And this, he did without first running it by the board, now six members strong with the election of Maynard Jackson and Washington transportation lawyer Berl Bernhard in July 1982. When Michael finally did get around to informing the board of his change in direction, no one objected.

"I would have been quite content going the distance, staying true the ideology of getting poor people on planes that had traditionally been reserved for middle and upper middle-class folks in suits and ties," says Kolber. "But Michael was more practical than I."

Indeed, the decision to abandon the low-fare model may have saved Air Atlanta from the dustbin of grand ideas.

CHAPTER 8

The heads-up that the discount airline model was fast becoming passé with investors had been a stunner for Michael, but hardly a show-stopper. He had already made it through the rigors of certification, had an itinerary of prospective investor meetings lined up and, as far as he could see, the skies overhead were still sunny and blue. This was no time for wringing of hands or abandoning ship. Michael simply went in another direction to find the hook with which Air Atlanta could snag investors.

There were only so many options in designing a new business model, given that there are just four things passengers care about: cost, schedules, safety, and service, though not necessarily in that order. Michael's alternative plan would have to keep fares in range of the going industry rates or else it would tempt an all-out war with major carriers, as other new carriers had learned the hard way. Air One, a regional service with flights from St. Louis to Newark, Dallas, Kansas City and Washington, D.C., had proven how dangerous undercutting existing rates can be. TransWorld Airlines, which dominated the St. Louis airport, counterpunched Air One's low fares with drastic cuts of its own, dropping fares so low that, at one point, a first class ticket on TWA was going for only $20 more than Air One's discounted coach fare. The upstart had no choice but to drop its rates too, a fiscally hazardous move that spooked investors who refused to cough up more money until Air One showed a profit. It never did.

Meanwhile, if Air Atlanta tried to undercut the big airlines through scheduling tactics, it could find itself with no runway or gate clearances – that's how serious the big boys were about beating back challengers.

Safety was non-negotiable, as all ordinary and extraordinary measures would be taken to ensure that Air Atlanta flights took off, flew and landed without incident, no matter how it branded itself. Michael invariably approved expenditures for personnel, processes, training or equipment to secure and enhance safety, no matter the cost.

With services as the only viable area for distinguishing the new airline from its competitors, Michael decided on upscale offerings for a new target customer. His would be the airline that catered to business travelers, making their flights more convenient, more comfortable and, by degrees, more luxurious than what they would experience for the same price on the major carriers. The pivot established Air Atlanta as the forerunner of a crop of commercial luxury airline carriers that would emerge some two decades later.

The new business plan he commissioned from Simat, Helliesen and Eichner opened the case for the new model by asserting that people who regularly fly for business purposes—a whopping 65 percent of short-distance travelers—were a neglected and unhappy bunch.

"They do not like crowded airplanes and facilities," the consultants reported, adding with no apparent sense of irony that business travelers were "particularly resentful of having to share the airline's attentions with people traveling at discounted fares"—the very people Michael's first business model had in mind.

Air Atlanta, it said, would offer at least four "well-timed" flights per day to nearby destinations with an emphasis on "reliable, efficient and friendly service in a distinctive four-abreast aircraft cabin." Michael planned to convert a fleet of Boeing 727-100 jets into essentially all first-class transports, reconfiguring the cabins so that they held 88 seats rather than the customary 125, thereby ensuring that each passenger would have an extraordinarily spacious seat next to either the aisle or window. In flight, passengers would be treated to grilled quail salad, chocolate-dipped strawberries and other gourmet appetizers to be served on real china, not plastic or paper plates. Their beverages would be served in crystal tumblers or stemware. They would dab their chins with linen napkins, not tissue-thin paper squares. Copies of the *Wall Street Journal* and popular business magazines would be provided at no additional cost. And the liquor would be free.

As its founder envisioned it, Air Atlanta would begin pampering its passengers as soon as they arrived at the terminal. A baggage valet would meet them at the counter to cart their carry-on luggage to the plane. A shuttle would take them from the check-in counter to their gates. If they had to wait for the flight, they could do so in a lovely, private lounge with free telephones and work space and upscale refreshments at their disposal. First class treatment all the way.

While no expense would be spared on features designed to win over traveling businessmen and women, Michael had every intention of saving where he could behind the scenes. Air Atlanta would take advantage of the surplus of experienced pilots, flight attendants and mechanics resulting from the Braniff Airlines collapse of 1982 and walk-offs at financially troubled and morale-challenged Continental Airlines. A pilot who might earn $90,000 on the major airlines would be paid $40,000 to fly for Air Atlanta. Flight attendants, typically earning $25,000 salaries elsewhere, would collect $14,000 a year from Air Atlanta. Mechanics, ticket agents and others would earn as little as half of what their counterparts earned at the big airlines. Like People Express with its plebeian profile, Air Atlanta would require employees to do more than one job and to acquire stock in the company. Its rationale was identical to People's: multi-tasking would increase efficiency and esprit de corps; stock ownership would inspire proprietary concern for the company.

Like People, the business-branded Air Atlanta would buy and retrofit used aircraft as a cost-saving measure. And like no-frills title-holder Southwest Airlines, Air Atlanta would employ a two-tier fare system with reduced rates between the business day's morning and afternoon rush hours and also on weekends.

"There was more political clout than there ever had been for African-Americans, but it was still a miracle that he was able to do it," says George

Dalley. "The fact that he chose to make his airline the luxury service, the upscale service that he did? When he told me that, I was amazed at his audacity. Others went with the low-fare model. But he had a bigger dream. Most of us dream big but have no way to squeeze it into reality. Michael Hollis found a way."

The drastically revised business model would be the only Air Atlanta that investors other than NAPFE would come to know. The others would never hear a pitch for the no-frills, low-fare model that Michael had initially proposed as a tool for leveling the playing field for the elite and the hoi polloi. Michael believed his new and unique niche model with its high-end face and low-budget underbelly would wow investors. With the new business plan in hand, the backing of a board stacked with influential business leaders, and a Certificate of Public Convenience and Necessity from the U.S. Civil Aeronautics Board, Michael had all the horsepower he needed to build his airline's fledgling portfolio. As always, he showed up loaded for bear, every bit as prepared to plunge into the weeds about load factors, block hours, code sharing, yield management and seat density as he was to hold court on the nuances of investment strategy and dividend projections. His ability to call up arcane details and statistics on the spot, his overall command of the subject matter and his undeniable self-confidence, enthusiasm and charm—all of it conveyed in calm, resonant tones—were captivating and he knew it.

His first score was the North Carolina Mutual Life Insurance Company, of Durham, North Carolina, founded by black businessmen in the 1890s. North Carolina Mutual was to Durham what Alonzo Herndon's insurance company had been to Atlanta – an ignition switch for black empowerment and enrichment. Michael would have loved to get financial support from the great Atlanta Life Insurance Company, but he and Maynard had quickly dispensed with that notion, realizing there was no chance of it happening. For one thing, Atlanta Life CEO Jesse Hill, Jr., was on Delta's board of directors; for another, Hill was hardly Maynard Jackson's biggest fan. There had always been an undercurrent of tension between the two, dating back to when Maynard bucked Hill's brethren at the Butler YMCA by jumping the line in the 1973 mayor's race.

Like his meeting with Robert White of NAPFE, Michael's introduction to North Carolina Mutual's William J. Kennedy was arranged by Maynard Jackson, whose relatives in Durham were long-time friends of Kennedy and his family. Through that connection, Jackson learned of the insurance company's investment profile and arranged for Michael to have an audience with Kennedy. The insurance executive was promptly impressed and North Carolina Mutual, the largest black life insurance company in the country, put up $200,000.

In turn, Kennedy shared the opportunity with his friend, Ed Duggar, president of Urban National Corporation, a venture capital fund based in Boston. Shortly after meeting with Michael, Urban National pitched in to the tune of $250,000.

Soon after their investments, both Kennedy and Duggar were elected to Air Atlanta's board of directors, an expanding cartel of powerful men who had either the authority or the connections to make things happen. Their selection as board members was in keeping with Michael's lifelong custom of befriending people in high places who could help him bypass intermediaries and go straight to the top – the president, not the chief of staff; the chairman of the board, not the treasurer; a named partner at the law firm, not a senior associate.

Accordingly, Duggar and Kennedy arranged a meeting for Michael with Frank Savage and Slivy Edmonds, two senior-level African-American executives at the Equitable Life Assurance Society of the United States, a goliath in the insurance industry. Savage had been a friend since Julius introduced him to Michael over cocktails at My Brother and Me, an upscale bar in downtown Washington, D.C., in the late 1970s.

The Equitable introductions put Michael in tall cotton and at a most opportune time. Like many major corporations in the early 1980s, Equitable was on the lookout for minority enterprises it could support. Black America was beginning to assert itself institutionally as well as socially, becoming increasingly more prominent in all levels of government, business and popular culture. The optics of a racially inclusive portfolio was useful to companies that had or hoped to attract significant black clientele and show that they were evolving with the times. Michael appreciated Equitable's insistence that its interest in Air Atlanta had naught to do with affirmative action or public relations but was solely based on its investment value, but he suspected that cultural pressures had played a role in getting the company's attention.

At the end of the day, however, motives behind a company's largesse were of little concern to a man anxious about getting his airline up and running. Equitable's $15 million was a resounding triumph for Michael and he and his team were elated, not only because of what they could do with that much money but also because of what it said to the rest of Wall Street—namely, that Air Atlanta was a worthy contender.

"What attracted us to him initially was his concept," an Equitable official told *The New York Times*. "It was one of the best thought-out and solidly researched business plans I had ever seen." The executive explained that his company did not normally involve itself in start-ups, "but this one struck us as having enormous potential for success."

With the help of another Jackson friend, the Corporate Responsibility Investment Committee of Aetna Insurance Company, another industry great, considered investing in Air Atlanta. "The airline industry is a challenging industry, even among the best," says Sandy Cloud, then chairman of the investment committee. "Michael's business plan made sense. With Atlanta as its base and Mayor Jackson's support, this thing had a chance to be really successful." Cloud said that, other than the normal due diligence, there was no resistance to the proposal. Aetna put in $5 million.

To entice investors and control its outlays, Air Atlanta issued zero coupon convertible bonds instead of stock. The bonds gave Air Atlanta the money it needed for operations immediately while deferring the payoff. An investor would write a check to Air Atlanta in exchange for a zero bond that would mature in later years for a pre-set rate of return on their investment.

The zero coupon bond was hardly new to the investment world, but it had never been used to secure funding for a major startup until Michael and his fellow financial whiz kids—Dan Kolber and Dartmouth classmate Gary Love, then a managing director at Kidder Peabody—figured out a way to manipulate it to raise capital for Air Atlanta. It was another example of the ingenuity and daring that was quickly becoming Michael's trademark – always pushing the envelope, flouting conventions and reinventing the wheel. As word got out, the phones rang constantly with entrepreneurs calling for advice on how to deploy the zero coupon bond.

The combination of Michael's know-how and Air Atlanta's expanding investment portfolio paved the way for other investors to follow Equitable and Aetna's lead. The National Bank of Georgia signed on for several million and the City of Atlanta allotted $1.5 million for Air Atlanta to improve its space at the city-owned airport.

"Monday through Friday, there were four or five appointments each day," recalls Kolber. "We'd go up to Wall Street, boom, boom, boom, boom. He would always start at the top; he would never come in mid-level. If he didn't know somebody, he would call up one of his contacts and say, 'Who do you know on So-and-So's board?' They'd say, 'I know the chairman,' and the next thing you know, we're in. They literally would not know what hit 'em."

Preparation was key. Years before Michael ever began canvassing the big leagues for capital, Atlanta investment banker T.M. Alexander, Jr., had taught him the importance of understanding the "home cooking" behind deal making and he never forgot it. Under Alexander's tutelage, Michael had learned to study the organization of Fortune 500 companies and chart the directors' relationships with one another so he could customize his pitches to fit the underlying dynamics.

"Michael could distill information and synthesize it and look ahead like a chess player," says Kolber. "You couldn't say no to Michael."

Of course, some did say no, only to be met by alternative proposals that, in more cases than not, resulted in either a change of heart, a promise to reconsider or, at the very least, an introduction to another powerbroker who was likely to buy in. If a prospect was clearly a dead-end, Michael would cut his losses quickly and move on to the next one. Dan Kolber recalls that, when Michael called Texas billionaire H. Ross Perot about backing Air Atlanta and Perot began filibustering, Michael pretended the phone line had gone bad and ended the conversation so he could go on to the next prospect.

Even though Air Atlanta was not proposing the discounted fares that invariably riled the major carriers, the big boys at Atlanta Hartsfield, Delta and Eastern, did not receive the incursion warmly. Not that Michael was surprised. Before deregulation, an airline's turf and prosperity were protected by the Civil Aeronautics Board. New entrants had to survive a wringer of hearings, offers of proof, and bureaucratic delays on top of incumbent carriers' objections. Deregulation had removed those safeguards and opened the door the new entrants, and opened it wide. The big carriers, accustomed as they were to ruling the roost, were bound to be unhappy with late-blooming competition, even a small carrier like Air Atlanta, which was not even pretending to take the majors on head-to-head. At many hubs, the majors pounced on the newcomers and clipped their wings by slicing fares, driving the startups to ground in relatively short order. Others tried to squash the newbies with an overwhelming show of capacity, like Braniff, which, in a single day in late 1978, added sixteen flights and thirty-two destinations to its itinerary to show its might—a very costly stroke of overkill considering how explosively fuel costs had risen.

But turf battles were to be expected. Delta had been flying passengers into and out of Atlanta since 1930, when it was still primarily a mail and cargo service. Atlanta had been its headquarters since 1941 and the city had watched Delta Airlines grow into a behemoth, introducing jet service, nonstop coast-to-coast flights and computerized reservation systems while occasionally swallowing up a competitor along the way.

For Atlanta, Delta meant thousands of jobs, a solid tax base, a corporate presence in civic affairs and charitable support. Many Atlantans took pride in the fact that one of the world's foremost airlines was based in their town, home of the world's busiest airport. The self-proclaimed "hometown airline" of Atlanta, Delta resented Michael's decision to name his airline after a city it had long claimed as its exclusive domain and it was none too happy that he had Mayor Jackson's blessings in doing so. Through back channels, Delta surrogates were dispatched to disable Air Atlanta's local fundraising efforts—a mission they seem to have accomplished, as none of Atlanta's major companies would invest so much as a dime in the upstart airline. The apparently orchestrated snubs only underscored Mayor Jackson's long-running lament that Atlanta's white business establishment "would sing glory hallelujah with you, while at the same time, socking it to you in the name of the Lord."

Yet outwardly, both Delta and Eastern took care not to look like they were bullying the new airline, especially since it was founded by a black man in the politically alert, predominantly black city that happened to be the founder's actual hometown. Although other big carriers had clobbered new competitors when they encroached on their hubs, neither Delta nor Eastern lowered its fares to torture the new airline. Besides, Air Atlanta had estimated that it would put only a seven percent dent in the big airlines' profits and, in fact, would help stave off "low-fare entrants that would do severe damage to majors' yields and profitability." Air Atlanta's negligible threat to incumbent airlines coupled with Michael's considerable political connections in the city and beyond may have accounted for Delta and Eastern holding their powder. But analysts believed that once Air Atlanta began turning a profit and growing, the tentative truce with Delta and Eastern would end.

The one area where Delta and Eastern openly refused to cooperate with the startup airline was the interline feature—the pact among airlines to incorporate one another's schedules, ticketing and baggage handling into their own systems for the sake of customer convenience and flight coordination. Try as it might, Air Atlanta could not forge an interline agreement with either of Atlanta's largest carriers. That would change the next year, when Georgia Republican Congressman Newt Gingrich stepped in to broker an interline deal for Air Atlanta with Delta and Eastern. Once again, Michael's knowing-someone-who-knew-someone would come to the rescue.

By January of 1984, Michael had raised $35 million for his new regional jet carrier—the most money any African-American entrepreneur in the U.S. had ever amassed to start a business. In addition, General Electric Credit Corporation had committed nearly $16 million for aircraft purchases from Pan American Airways. GE then leased the jets back to Air Atlanta under a seven-year agreement.

Lucky for Pan Am that one of the world's newest airlines had come along when it had. Expecting its business to remain on the uptick, the self-proclaimed "world's most experienced airline" had ordered several new wide-bodied jets to expand its international capacity and replace its fleet of fuel-hungry, narrow-bodied jets like the Boeing 727 models. But after deregulation, other major U.S. carriers began testing Pan Am's lucrative international waters and gave it a run for its money, leaving the carrier with a bloated inventory and rising overhead. It needed to unload.

As part of its sales deal with Air Atlanta, Pan Am restored each plane to top condition and painted the aircraft in Air Atlanta's gray, blue and burgundy color scheme. United Airlines was contracted to renovate the interiors to the new airline's specifications: a first class cabin with five rows of four seats—two on either side of the aisle; a coach cabin containing sixty-eight seats, all of them wider than usual, with two on one side of the aisle and three on the other; new carpeting and lighting; larger storage compartments; and upgraded galleys and lavatories. Air Atlanta also signed with Pan Am to handle its reservations and to provide ongoing maintenance services for the planes. Sweetening the deal, Pan Am threw in $600,000 worth of training for eighteen cockpit crews, one-hundred-forty-four flight attendants and forty mechanics and dispatchers at no additional cost.

In addition to aircraft, Air Atlanta's new millions were spent on gate fees; insurance; amenities; salaries and benefits for pilots, flight attendants, agents, ground crews and administrators; fuel; maintenance; monthly leasing fees; and mandatory test flights. As it prepared for its first scheduled flights, Air Atlanta had about three million dollars in the bank, enough to cover about three months of operations.

On January 15, 1984, as Air Atlanta prepared for takeoff, ads heralding the advent of a new airline "born to serve business" appeared in the Sunday editions of *The New York Times*, the *Memphis Commercial Appeal* and the *Atlanta Journal-Constitution* and on local TV stations in Memphis and Atlanta. Designed by a Virginia advertising firm, the ads depicted an Air Atlanta jet emerging from a broken egg shell, as if newly hatched. The ad touted the special services for "the hassled business flyer tired of being overlooked and underserved."

The bait had been cast. In two weeks, Air Atlanta would know if the fish were biting.

CHAPTER 9

Early on February 1, 1984, a brisk and sunny day in Atlanta, two immaculate 727s sat on the tarmac at Hartsfield International, preening in the morning light. Scores of well-dressed men and women had gathered in a smartly adorned gate lounge inside the terminal and passersby could see that they were in high spirits, merrily clinking glasses of champagne and smiling brightly as they awaited Air Atlanta's inaugural flight. A few pressed against the plate glass windows to get a better look at the sleek, spit-shined aircraft outside—the hard, undeniable proof of a young, black Atlanta native's outsized dream brought to life. Michael Hollis had built an airline, just as he said he would.

Former skeptics and true believers alike rejoiced, smothering Michael with laudatory slaps on the back, hugs, and kisses as he worked his way through the joyous crowd. Virginia Hollis beamed with delight as well-wishers congratulated her on her youngest child's fait accompli. In a town where entrepreneurship is de rigueur, this was something extraordinary. Michael had accomplished what no other African-American ever had, not only in Atlanta but nationwide: He had created a first-rate passenger airline. And he was barely 30 years old.

The week preceding the inaugural passenger flights had been hectic yet productive for Air Atlanta's officials and staff as they tended to the hundreds of small details that would stamp the airline with the distinguishing touches Michael had promised. At a press preview that week, reporters noted that the glass-partitioned private gate lounge was still barren; the carpeting, furnishings and decorative pieces were not yet in place. Robert Henderson, the airline's vice president of human resources, had assured them it would all get done in time and he was right. On opening day, comfortable leather chairs and mahogany tables with beige telephones posed on new gray carpeting. Tasteful artworks adorned the walls. Silver urns of hot coffee and delicate teapots stood at the ready next to porcelain cups and saucers.

If the adrenaline rush of starting a new airline had not been enough to keep Air Atlanta's executives energized and excited, then face time with the president of the United States surely had. Ronald Reagan had come to town in late January for a pro-business rally sponsored by the U.S. Chamber of Commerce, the Atlanta Chamber and one of Air Atlanta's investors, the National Bank of Georgia. During his speech, the president lauded Air Atlanta as an exemplar of "the spirit of free enterprise" – priceless recognition for even the most reputable company; a stupendous endorsement for a brand-new venture. "I'm pleased to say that we're getting the federal government out of the way so that they can compete," the president boasted, notwithstanding the fact that deregulation – "getting the federal government out of the way" – was enacted before he took office.

Following Reagan's address to the invitation-only crowd, he and Michael met privately and strummed a chord of kinship by noting their mutual ties to General Electric, the investor that financed Air Atlanta's new planes. Then an actor, Reagan had been the host of GE's popular weekly radio and TV show and was the company's celebrity pitchman back in the 1950s and '60s. He and Michael joked that they both owed their success to General Electric.

Michael gave his new friend a model Air Atlanta 727 inscribed with "Spirit of America" – the rally's theme. He also gave the president a gold card for Air Atlanta's version of the frequent flyer program, making the leader of the free world the first member of the Founders' Club. A few months later, President Reagan would send a note to Michael thanking him for the card, adding "I thought I should give you something in return." A personally autographed photograph of the 40th president accompanied the note.

Michael could not have had much sleep before the biggest day of his life. The night before, he had celebrated the impending launch with yet another party, this one for 300 business and civic leaders hosted by Mayor Andrew Young. The celebration had been the last of a series that had begun weeks before – parties for friends and family, parties for investors and for city officials, parties for contractors, and parties for travel agents whose patronage would be key to Air Atlanta's bookings. If the festivities had taken a toll, it didn't show on this day, when Michael was buoyant in his dual role as host and man of the hour. He moved through the excited crowd with assurance and ease, soaking up the glory and praise heaped upon him by the throng of well-wishers that had come to witness the new airline's inauguration and, in many cases, to take one of its first flights. Reporters and photographers from the *Wall Street Journal* and *The New York Times* joined the swarm of local newspapers and television stations trailing Michael through the crowded lounge and interviewed several of the celebrants, especially Michael's ebullient mother. It was just the kind of bootstraps story their readers, viewers, and listeners loved and they devoured Mrs. Hollis' sweet recollections about Michael's upbringing and the early indicators that he, like his airline, was born for business.

After an hour or so of mingling and schmoozing, the group was directed to the tarmac. Yards of wide yellow ribbon encircled the stairs to one of the planes. A lectern and several chairs were cordoned off for dignitaries who would participate in the brief dedicatory ceremonies. Mayor Young had proclaimed February 1st "Air Atlanta Day" and now, joined by Michael, Georgia Governor Joe Frank Harris, and several members of the Atlanta City Council, the mayor smiled broadly as he stepped onto the podium, pausing for the cameras.

More than once, Young had let Michael and Julius know that he thought they were too ambitious for their age and inexperience. More patience and more modest dreams would serve them well, he had counseled. The Hollis brothers heard Young's admonitions and understood the mayor's cautiousness. But it was not enough to deter them. If they failed, it would be on them, they argued. All they wanted from Young was for him to keep the doors open so they could try.

The brothers' insistence on pushing ahead with Air Atlanta would be a burr in the new mayor's side as he pursued his own plan for building the city's business portfolio, largely by attracting international investments to Atlanta. Young promised to help pull strings at the city-controlled airport to ensure that Air Atlanta had the accommodations it needed, but Michael's new airline was clearly not a priority. Had it not been for his allegiance to Maynard Jackson, who had pushed Young as his successor, the mayor might have let some of his promises fall through the cracks. It had been Jackson and Julius' job to keep the pressure on the headstrong mayor and, when all was said and done, Young had come through. At the ribbon-cutting that February morning, he didn't seem at all like the half-hearted supporter who had caused so much anxiety for Michael and his team in the months prior. That day, Mayor Young seemed as keyed up about Air Atlanta as anyone else.

"Air Atlanta is a welcome new member of our business community," Young said. "The airline will create jobs and contribute to the economic growth of Atlanta, the State of Georgia and the southeastern region of the United States."

Julius watched as his former boss basked in the limelight before boarding the first plane bound for Memphis. Julius had intended to take one of the flights himself, but since he and Michael were determined that every aspect of inauguration day would be flawless, he remained behind to make sure that things were in order for the flights' eventual return to Hartsfield.

Michael took the New York flight because he and Kolber had set up a couple of meetings for later that day in midtown Manhattan. Now that his airline was reality and no longer mere theory, he was only more confident about his pitch to investors and would delight in telling them that Air Atlanta had brought him to the city that day. The men he would meet with on Wall Street would find him to be his usual all-about-business self, but on the flight up, it was his charm and hospitality that would be remembered. Throughout the flight, he walked up and down the aisles checking on his passengers' comfort, sharing light jokes and thanking them for their support. His mood couldn't have been better and it showed in his quick laugh, light-hearted banter and the sure-footed, upright way he strolled through the plane. All of the difficulties and challenges of the past two years seemed to have been left behind as the jet soared into the sunny blue sky.

Once the flight landed smoothly at JFK, Virginia Hollis, her daughter Elaine and James Bernard's wife, Pat, were surprised to find a limousine waiting to whisk them into Manhattan. Michael had made special arrangements for them at the famed Tavern on the Green in Central Park so they could enjoy a leisurely luncheon of haute cuisine while he made his rounds on Wall Street. Mrs. Hollis couldn't believe it. Here she was, a woman who had once earned a living by serving plates of smothered chicken and collard greens to hungry diners, now being treated as an honored guest at a legendary restaurant in one of the world's most exciting cities. She, Elaine and Pat giggled like schoolgirls on the ride there – that is, until she got wind of the pricey menu awaiting her. Ever the frugal one, Mrs. Hollis announced that the outing, though bound to be lovely, was an unwarranted extravagance even if Michael was paying for it. Nearing the restaurant, she directed the chauffeur to pull over to the curb where the three elegantly dressed women promptly exited the limo and queued up at one of the city's ubiquitous food carts, ordering New York-style hot dogs with all the fixings. Neither Elaine nor Pat objected. As excited as they were, anything would have tasted good that day.

Upon their return to Atlanta in late afternoon, the passengers were again treated to refreshments and other small comforts and mementos in the fancy new gate lounge. Julius had seen to it that everything from food to furnishings had been refreshed so that travelers would have yet one more thing to talk about. Good word-of-mouth would be important to a new airline whose limited advertising budget was being gobbled up by expensive ad buys in the New York, Atlanta and Memphis markets.

Michael was relieved to have the first runs behind him. He luxuriated in the day's ovations and the satisfaction of how near-perfect it all had been. The years of brainstorming, researching, planning, organizing, and raising capital had paid off in spades and everyone was talking about him as Atlanta's newest and most accomplished Boy Wonder. As the last guests departed Hartsfield, Michael gathered his team to debrief about the day's events and to discuss plans for the next day when the press, dignitaries, and yellow ribbons would be gone and Air Atlanta would face its first normal day of operations with paying customers. The schedule called for five non-stop, roundtrip flights departing Atlanta for New York, where international passengers could connect to Pan Am flights; and four non-stop roundtrips from Atlanta to Memphis. Four times a day, Air Atlanta flights would fly from New York to Memphis and vice versa, before returning to Atlanta.

The team was happy to find that all seemed ready for Day Two; everything was "in table order," as Mrs. Hollis would put it. The airline still had a few logistical hitches to work out, like interline agreements with Delta and Eastern, but Michael was confident that those would come in time, especially since he had taken care to nurture friendships with the top men at both carriers and had been diligent about keeping his high-level contacts on call in case he needed them to make things happen. It bugged him that his new airline had only three million dollars in the bank – barely enough to sustain a few months of expenses, which included GE's leasing fees of $57,000 a month per plane. But he wouldn't let that put too much of a damper on his spirits, not with his well-tested talent for talking people into writing big checks. Not with E.F. Hutton having prepared a prospectus to sell one million shares of Air Atlanta stock at $22 a share and an April date for the public offering. As much as he would rather not operate so close to the edge, the challenge invigorated him. One way or another, the money would come.

If he had any regrets at all, it was that his great friend, mentor, and father figure Dr. Benjamin Mays was unable to take part in the opening day festivities. Michael had stopped by Dr. Mays' house the day before to brief him on the inaugural plans and give him a press kit. He found his revered mentor in his sickbed, where he had been grappling with a long-running illness and, at 89, the infirmities of old age. It would be one of their last times together. The brilliant educator and civil rights champion died at an Atlanta hospital two months later.

Although Michael knew his dear friend was nearing the end of his days, Dr. Mays' death hit him hard. He had known and loved the man all of his life. Benjamin Mays had been more of a father to him than his own. His wise counsel had informed him, inspired him, propelled him. His perseverance, intelligence, and faith had been the model for how Michael would deal with adversity and good fortune alike. He had been Socrates to Michael's Plato. And now, he was gone.

A few days after Dr. Mays passed, the *Atlanta Constitution* published Michael's tribute to his dear departed friend titled "The Day a Student and His Teacher Graduated." As part of his own laudation to Mays, Congressman Gingrich read Michael's tribute into the *Congressional Record*. It recapitulated Benjamin Mays' longing to attend Dartmouth and the honorary degree that had been bestowed upon him at Michael's behest. In the piece, Michael confessed that he had only recently come to appreciate Dr. Mays' oft-stated philosophy that everyone has a unique purpose that no one else can fulfill.

"These reflections are penned as I sit in an airborne Air Atlanta Boeing 727 jet," he wrote, suggesting that founding an airline was his special calling.

He ended the article with the kind of tender poetic touch that his many business associates rarely witnessed except when Michael was talking about, or talking to, his mother.

"As I look out on a glorious spring and blue horizon, it occurs to me that my hero, Dr. Benjamin E. Mays is not really gone," he wrote. "The man with the wise eyes and soft smile is watching us from the other side of yonder clouds."

CHAPTER 10

It should come as no surprise that a young man bold enough to stride into the sequestered suites of some of the most powerful business moguls in the country and talk them out of millions of their dollars would have no compunction about propositioning an attractive woman from whom the rewards are far more personal and perhaps just as exhilarating.

Michael was a ladies' man. His sexual appetite was as big, constant and insatiable as his hunger for capital and venturesome business deals. In both cases, the seduction appeared to be as alluring and satisfying as the conquest or consummation itself. Whether hitting on women or making a pitch to investors, Michael was always prepared for a "yes" but he was seldom dispirited if he heard otherwise. If a woman rebuffed his advances, he would continue talking to her as if he never had any intention other than to make small talk and strike up a friendship. Sometimes the seamless segue would work an enchantment of its own and the charmed woman would end up at Michael's table, or in his bed, anyway.

Dan Kolber recalls a funny instance in New York City that exemplified his friend's intrepidity about approaching women. They were walking down a crowded street when Michael spotted an attractive woman up ahead. He stepped up his pace to catch up with her.

"You are a beautiful woman," he said to the startled stranger. "How would you like...."

Just then, a man pushed forward and inserted himself between Michael and the woman, putting his arm around her waist as if to stake a claim. Without skipping a beat, Michael stopped and extended his hand. "Hi, I'm Michael Hollis," he said. "I just launched a new airline and we're celebrating. Would you all like to join us?" A few minutes later, Michael, Dan, and the couple were laughing raucously and ordering drinks on Michael's tab at a Manhattan bar.

"He didn't give a damn what the response might be," said Todd Alexander, Michael's frequent wing man in those years. "It was clearly a game to him and he found it as amusing as most of the women he was targeting."

Several years younger than Michael, Todd was single and good-looking and, like his friend, intent on taking full advantage of those attributes. He had known Michael since he was a kid, when Michael would sit around with his father, T. M. Alexander, Jr., and he and his sister Kim would listen in as their dad and Michael sipped wine and talked politics, sports, and business. Occasionally, their grandfather, the venerable T.M. Alexander,

Sr.—the real estate magnate and one of the Auburn Avenue godfathers—would be there too, adding a touch of history and gravitas to the setting.

When Todd and Kim's father was killed in a boating accident in Honduras in 1983, the tragedy hit Michael especially hard. He drew even closer to the Alexander family to comfort them and help mentor Todd and Kim.

Now, as trusted friends and unattached men in a city chockfull of available women, Michael and Todd moved about like kings of the hill, sizing up their options at bars, clubs, restaurants and other gatherings in Atlanta. Todd looked for beauty, confidence, and class. But none of those seemed to matter much to Michael.

"Attractive was defined solely by what Michael deemed attractive," Todd said. "There wasn't an age, race, physical type or demographic that was out of the question or off the table. Whether it was the 21-year-old waitress at Houston's or a popular local professional hockey player's sister in her 50s, he was all in."

So confident was Michael that he didn't even bother to concoct a killer opening line for his approaches, relying instead on the quaint compliment— "You're so pretty" or "You have such beautiful eyes"—to let a woman know that he found her appealing and that he might be interested in getting to know her better. Todd enjoyed watching him work his magic.

"I'll never forget we went out to dinner together with two female friends he had scared up," Todd says. "We were meeting the two ladies there and shortly after we arrived, in they walked wearing some crazy, scandalous gear. I looked at Michael as if to say, 'Where in the hell did you find these freaks?' He just smiled and said, 'It's okay' and proceeded to greet them with prolonged hugs and cheek kisses." After a few rounds of champagne and lobster, Todd noticed that a prominent Atlanta lawyer was dining at a neighboring table with his daughter, who was a former classmate of Todd's. He could sense their astonishment at finding the two men – one, a scion of one of the city's most respected families; the other, the toast of Atlanta – keeping company with women who seemed to be costumed as street walkers. For a moment, he wished that he could vaporize right there and then.

"About two months later, I ended up seeing one of those women again on my birthday," Todd recalls. "Michael had arranged to have her meet me for a drink in private." Michael got a kick out of throwing his friends for a loop. He found it hilarious to place a close friend in an awkward situation and watch him or her squirm. At Kim's wedding, for example, Michael brought along the groom's former girlfriend as his date. Years would pass before Kim could laugh about that, but Michael immediately found it hilarious. His prankishness never crossed over into the dangerous, but he liked to play to the edge and push his friends' buttons.

None of Michael's family was surprised to hear that Michael did not always exercise discretion when it came to women. As much as they didn't like it, they tolerated it as one of the eccentricities that spring from exceptional minds. Besides, he was a grown man; it was his life. And it wasn't as though there hadn't been relationships with accomplished, well-mannered women. For a while, Michael dated broadcaster Robin Roberts; and, before everyone in the world knew who she was, Oprah Winfrey used to pop into town and sit in Michael's office, sometimes for hours, until he finished his business and could turn his attentions to her. Still, the booty-shaking, bosom-bearing, heavily made-up, round-the-way girl was not an unusual companion for the distinguished chairman of Air Atlanta, at least not in private. When it came to his business circle, he tended to make the social rounds alone, both to stifle gossip and to be unencumbered in the event a new lovely caught his eye.

Only rarely did Michael appear to be serious about a romance. While in law school at the University of Virginia, he had fallen in love with pre-med student Gail Bryant, so much so that he asked her to marry him. To his chagrin, Gail wasn't ready yet for that big a move; she wanted to finish med school and get her residency behind her first. They continued to see each other for several more years, but Michael never asked her again and the two drifted apart.

A few years later, he met Neysa Dillard, a senior at Spelman College, and the two struck up a romance. Michael's family liked the pairing and several members of his family believed the couple was headed toward marriage.

"He made sure I was treated like a queen," Neysa recalls, noting that all of their many outings together were "first class all the way" – the best restaurants, the best travel accommodations, the best seats in the house. Though impressed, Neysa says she understood that Michael was not putting on airs for her; his style represented his insistence on top quality provisions as much as it did his affections for her. "It wasn't showy," she says. "He just believed that's what people deserved."

Tightly focused on her career in healthcare administration, Neysa went to Michigan for graduate school and worked there for several years afterward. Michael was in Atlanta. The separation slowly unraveled the romance, but not the friendship, which endured to the end. She eventually married a well-known broadcast executive and had two sons.

"I don't know if everyone saw the soft side to him," said Neysa. "A big kindness, a big heart. He was very passionate about his friends and his family, very much so. I felt very blessed to be one of those he cared about."

A few years would pass before Michael settled into another serious relationship. In the meantime, he busied himself with a long line of party girls, waitresses and store clerks who everyone knew would command Michael's attention only briefly, never long-term.

"I would go over to Michael's for food and drinks and there would be a new face and I would deftly ask Michael, 'Who the hell is that?'" Todd recalled. "He would tell me that they met at the grocery store or some other craziness and then he would stark chuckling."

For a time, Michael got hot and heavy with an exotic-looking Louisiana beauty who had been turning heads across Atlanta. She seemed to be crazy about him, so much so that she commissioned a larger-than-life-sized portrait of Michael, which he duly hung in his living room for all to see.

One night, Michael had a group of male friends over for poker and drinks and the men started speaking in uncensored, licentious language about women they had known or hoped to know. Unbeknownst to Michael, his girlfriend had hidden in a nearby closet and was absorbing all the sordid details, apparently growing more and more agitated with each crude tidbit as the men guffawed and slapped their knees. Suddenly, she burst from the closet, tore past Michael and ran into the kitchen where she pulled a sharp knife from the butcher block and began slashing the giant portrait. The night ended with embarrassment and mess galore, but without injury or police involvement. Even then, it took time for Michael to cut ties with the woman, who was rumored to be a practitioner of black magic. He didn't believe in those things but found it prudent to be patient with those who did. His friends would never stop laughing and teasing Michael about that night. For once, the master prankster had gotten his due.

It's only ironic that Michael could be so cavalier and mischievous in his private life, considering how carefully he managed his public image. In the business and civic realms, he was a vision of sophistication and refinement, with all the accouterments that entails. With a salary of $75,000 a year from Air Atlanta—the equivalent of about $175,000 in today's dollars—Michael maintained a fashionable condo at the Landmark in downtown Atlanta. He drove a Jaguar. He wore Brooks Brothers suits and custom-made, monogrammed shirts from Neiman Marcus. He entertained often and extravagantly, serving vintage wines and gourmet meals catered by top-notch chefs, if not prepared by the host himself.

"Their grandmother, Dear, taught both Julius and Michael the art of cooking," says older brother, Flem. "And they loved it. They especially loved cooking for family and friends."

Michael could be as particular and demanding about food as he was about the fine print in a business deal. Invariably, the simple act of placing an order at a restaurant involved a ritual that would keep the wait staff on pins and needles and his dinner companions amused.

"Michael would go over the menu with a fine-toothed comb," recalled Jeanne Simkins Hollis, Julius' wife. Julius had met Jeanne in 1981 at one of George and Pearl Dalley's great dinner parties in Washington, D.C., around the time the Reagan Administration moved to town. Jeanne, a beautiful young lawyer, had arrived on the arm of a FAA official that night but was seated next to Julius for dinner. When she learned that Julius was preparing to return to his hometown, Jeanne offered to introduce him to her unmarried cousin in Atlanta. But it was Jeanne who had captured Julius' imagination and, not long after, he invited her over for dinner. As the story goes, she was two hours late, he was nonchalant about her tardiness, she was impressed by his patience and understanding, a romance blossomed and in June 1986, they were married in her native North Carolina. Jeanne and her new brother-in-law became fast friends.

"Michael would ask the waiter, 'What about this; what's in that?'" Jeanne recalls fondly. "The final thing would be, 'Could you add some capers?' You knew you had a good 15 minutes to go while he quizzed them."

Todd Alexander says Michael's dining out ritual was something to behold.

"He would always ask the waiter for a sample of anything that piqued his curiosity on the menu," Todd says. "He would load them up by asking how it was prepared, then riddle them with questions until finally, if it sounded to his liking, he would just say, 'Can you bring me just a little sample of that? I just want to taste it to see if I want to order it.' It didn't matter if it was soup, wine, or steak; if it sounded good, he was going to sample it."

To Michael, good food was both a pleasurable indulgence and a tool for business. Every now and then, he would call Kim Alexander with an urgent request for one of her signature dishes so he could impress a guest he was having over to discuss business.

"When he was in the throes of a deal, he'd call and say, 'Kim, make a quiche so I can serve it to Maynard' or the other prominent guests at the meeting." Take-out or run-of-the-mill fare would never do. Nor would the disposable goods that many bachelors prefer.

"He was definitely not the Wal-Mart shopper," Kim says, laughing at the memory.

As Michael's ersatz kid sister, Kim adored him for his brilliant mind, ribald sense of humor and devotion to her family, particularly after her father's death. When she was in law school at Georgetown, Michael helped her finish a paper on the Supreme Court decision in *Bakke v. California*, the ruling that limited racial quotas in college admissions. She earned a high grade.

"It was just great to be my age and be around him with all he knew and understood," Kim said. "He was a tremendous son to his mother, and he was dedicated to his friends."

In addition to business opportunities, good food, good wine, good music and good sex, a new object captured Michael's affections in the early 1980s—something he discovered by happenstance. Just for the heck of it, he had taken up a college friend's offer to spend some down time at his family's vacation home on Hilton Head Island, South Carolina, a resort community known for its quiet, scenic beauty, ocean views, and tournament-level golf courses. Almost immediately, Michael fell in love with the island and soon bought a place of his own there where he could stare into the Atlantic and let his troubles wash out with the evening tide.

"I think Hilton Head was a great setting for him to think outside the box, which is what he did as well as, if not better, than anyone I've ever met," says Todd. "I think in Atlanta, he was constantly surrounded by people, places and things that made it more difficult to think outside of the city limits. Hilton Head may as well have been Zurich because he was comfortable and relaxed there and got a kick out of being on the phone talking business while staring out at the water. Hilton Head gave him that space he needed to constantly think big."

Life was good for Michael. Back home in Atlanta, he was the celebrated hometown prodigy invited to every A-list reception, gala, banquet, and party that kept the city's richest and most powerful on the move night after night. He was in constant demand to deliver keynote addresses to students, business leaders, and civil rights groups. Every other month or so, another national or local publication featured a glowing profile of the wunderkind from Atlanta's West End.

"Who is this grandstanding financing wizard?" *Forbes* magazine asked in an article titled "The Wings of Michael Hollis." Even though the article pointed out some of the potholes in Air Atlanta's financial runway—"The carrier … is losing money very fast," *Forbes* reported—its author joined other journalists in portraying Michael as something of a savant for making a go of a niche airline in a city dominated by two of the country's largest commercial carriers.

Indeed, Michael was proving that he was no flash in the pan. Money continued to come his way as he constantly talked to friends in high places, met with financiers, digested and analyzed stock market trends and business news, and stayed on the lookout for new sources of revenue. He was accustomed to being on the make but still hoped that a proposed public offering would allow him to slow the pace a bit after having raised tens of millions to get Air Atlanta off the ground. E.F. Hutton, one of the country's most respected stock brokerage firms, had agreed to underwrite an offering and had registered it with the U.S. Securities and Exchange Commission and created a prospectus. The plan called for the sale of one million preferred and common shares of Air Atlanta stock with an antici-pated yield of $20-22 million. The sale was scheduled for April 1984, two months after the airline's launch.

But recent industry events had made Hutton skittish. Another start-up, Air Florida, had recently filed for bankruptcy, Continental was on the skids, Eastern was bleeding money, and Air Atlanta was still wet behind the ears. The underwriter got cold feet and called off the stock sale.

Michael and Kolber raced to the Hutton offices in New York in a last-ditch effort to salvage the public offering. As usual, they went straight to the top, where they argued that the sale would be productive and reminded Hutton of the faith that heavy hitters like Equitable and Aetna had already bestowed upon Air Atlanta, as evidenced by their multi-million-dollar investments. The Hutton execs wouldn't budge. Maybe later, they said; but not now.

"Most people would say, 'Ok, we'll come back in six months,' but that wasn't how Michael operated," Kolber explains. "He would say, 'Ok, you're not ready to underwrite us now, but what would it take?' They would be vague. He would get them to be precise. Remember, this is a guy who never just accepted 'no.'

"They'd say, 'You need another $10 million to make the offer viable.' Michael would say, 'So, if I get four people to say they would give us $2.5 million each, would that work?' They'd get uncomfortable because Michael had put them on the spot. He would keep pressing them and they would say, 'Yeah, that would work.' So, then we'd camp out in their offices. Michael would find a pretty secretary and kind of flirt with her and then ask, 'Is there an office I could borrow? Maybe someone on vacation?' And, sure enough, she'd set us up in some office and he would have me write a letter on the spot: 'Dear Michael, we enjoyed meeting with you today. This will confirm what I told you during our meeting.' And we'd put in the part about raising $10 million at $2.5 million a pop being acceptable. And we'd put it on E.F. Hutton letterhead with the CEO's name on the signature line. I'd always add a line about 'nothing in this letter is binding.' Then we'd head out to potential investors in the city with the letter—sometimes I'd have to go to Columbia Circle and buy a suit on the way—and say, 'Look, Hutton is going to underwrite a public offering' and that would convince them to give us the money."

It was an impetuous, almost devil-may-care way to raise money, but it was Michael's way and, often enough, it worked. He understood that real estate may be all about location, location, location, but when it comes to raising capital, the name of the game is leverage. If he had to toy with the process in order to accomplish that, so be it.

Michael deployed other negotiating strategies too, says Kolber. "It wasn't just what he was going to give the target. He put just as much thought into what he was *not* going to give them at that first meeting. For example, the target would ask about something and Michael's answer would be, 'Well, we have a position paper on that and I'll send it to you.' That would accomplish three things: it would guarantee a follow-up, it would show that Michael would do what he promised, and it would show how thorough and perfect his preparation was."

Although the public offering fell through, Michael once again proved himself to be a master salesman. He would turn first to his early investors who, having already pumped millions into Air Atlanta, added $14 million more to the company coffers in mid-1984. Part of Michael's modus operandi was to shower his investors with praise and promise, catering to their egos and air of magnanimity, and underscoring their crucial role in his airline's success.

In a letter to the COO of General Electric Credit Corporation in late September 1984, Michael referenced an August speech in which he had extolled GECC's "courage" in financing Air Atlanta's initial fleet.

What I need is a continuation of that courage and faith shown in me. I am, as well as our nearly 400 employees are, counting on you and the credit corporation. Gary, we won't let you down!! We will deliver on our promise. We will make you proud.

With active faith,

Michael Hollis

One month later, Air Atlanta announced another new infusion of $9 million from Equitable, Aetna, and GECC. And Michael was in talks with other new prospects who had expressed interest in investing.

He had accomplished this despite a significant upset at the young airline that might have made investors second guess their decision had

Michael not been able to pass off the ordeal as "growing pains." From early on, CEO Rodney Brandt had complained that Michael meddled in the airline's operations, contradicting or overriding his own actions and decisions as CEO. Months of rankled nerves and hard feelings came to a head at the July 9, 1984 board meeting, where Brandt protested that Michael's job was to raise capital for the airline and, in his role as chairman of the board, to set the tone for policy and objectives. The day-to-day operations were, Brandt insisted, his province and his alone.

Brandt buttressed his position with a *Harvard Business Review* article on the best ways for growing companies to organize their leadership; and a consultant's report about Air Atlanta. He also presented a five-page letter proposing that he resign by no later than July 15th because, it said, he could no longer function in a company with "dual leadership." He gave a copy of each document to the directors.

Whether or not the resignation letter was a bluff and despite Brandt's attempt to persuade the board to side with him, Michael remained calm. He had anticipated this and had already spoken privately with each board member about Brandt's disgruntlement and what he saw as their irreconcilable differences. According to the minutes of that day's meeting, "[Michael] stated that he thought no purpose would be served by responding on a point-by-point basis to Mr. Brandt's criticism of the organizational structure of the company. He thanked Mr. Brandt for his contribution to the company."

The board went into executive session, but only as a formality. If Brandt thought his letter and arguments would spark debate or hesitation among the directors, it only proved how little he understood Michael Hollis. The board had already been primed to accept Brandt's resignation immediately, and to authorize Michael to negotiate a severance agreement. As orchestrated, it appointed Ronald Sapp, the company's chief financial officer, as acting president and general manager and crowned Michael as CEO, preempting any future claims of usurpation. All of it had been pre-arranged through Michael's one-on-ones with the various directors. Shortly thereafter, two other top executives quit, citing the same grievances, and were promptly replaced. Again, Michael had greased the skids beforehand. Categorically and unanimously, his board was behind him.

Despite being Michael's main collaborator, his right-hand man, and his confidante – and despite being a titled executive with Air Atlanta – Dan Kolber was still living in New York, having resisted Michael's continuous entreaties to move to Atlanta. As a husband and new father, he needed job security. Granted, Michael had covered his expenses for the frequent trips to Atlanta and had been paying him a salary all along, but Kolber wanted to make sure the airline was on solid ground before uprooting his family and abandoning his legal career. But between Michael's prodding and Lesley's unhappiness with her husband's overloaded work life and constant travel, the ground was beginning to give.

"Once he was in a position to pay me, he did. I think it was like $2,000 a month," Kolber says. "My salary at Weil, Gotshal in 1978 was $28,000 [about $106,000 today], the highest starting salary on Wall Street for lawyers at the time." The cost of living in Atlanta was much lower and good housing with backyards and space for a growing family was much more affordable. A $24,000 salary in Atlanta (about $91,000 today) would go a lot farther than a $28,000 salary in Manhattan. Besides, like Michael, Kolber craved something gutsier than practicing law.

Just before Thanksgiving 1984, Kolber, his wife, toddler son and infant daughter bid farewell to New York and moved to Atlanta.

CHAPTER 11

Like all of Virginia Robinson Hollis' children, Michael was polite, friendly and a paragon of southern charm. But he also knew how to exploit those traits to his advantage in business, believing that the personal touch only sweetened the pot. That tactic may have had as much to do with Delta and Eastern's refusal to use their wherewithal to hammer Air Atlanta into oblivion as did any public relations concerns over their treatment of an earnest upstart. Michael had schmoozed both Delta's David Garrett and Eastern's Frank Borman and converted them into friendly rivals. As a result, the airlines had thrown only nettlesome hitches in Air Atlanta's way – far away gates, which Air Atlanta worked around by creating the shuttle bus service; and their refusal to sign interline agreements, which cost Air Atlanta some bookings, but would not break its back. They could have repeated what TWA had done to Air One in St. Louis. They didn't.

When it came to his extensive, ever-expanding Rolodex of business contacts, Michael seldom missed an opportunity to congratulate, console, encourage or welcome a friend when something significant happened in their professional or private lives. Treating them as more than business associates was elemental to his charm offensive, so handwritten notes and personal phone calls were constantly being launched from his Atlanta office as occasions arose. Michael understood that if and when he needed help, the relationships he had cultivated would at least give his friends pause about turning him down.

Typifying the method, a letter from Michael to a major financier gushed with flattery and congratulations for the man's new position as head of an international finance firm and his impending move to the company's headquarters in Chicago. He thanked the man for "going to bat" for him with General Electric over the fleet financing for Air Atlanta. He talked about assembling other high-powered businessmen to welcome the executive to his new hometown. He mused about accompanying his friend on a trip to the company's offices overseas where, he fawned, the man would surely be greeted with honor and acclaim.

A few months later, when Michael learned his friend was coming to Atlanta, he pulled out all the stops and hosted a black-tie soiree in his honor. The guest list comprised the crème de la crème of Atlanta business and civic society. Afterward, Michael, the guest of honor, and a small party of friends retreated to a bar where they drank away what was left of the evening. By the time the night ended, Michael had extracted a multi-million-dollar pledge from his friend.

But the next day, the financier sent Michael a telegram excusing himself from any promises he may have made the night before, noting that he had had too much to drink and therefore should not be held to any sweet nothings he might have whispered in an inebriated state. Kolber laughed it off. "Easy come, easy go," he said. But Michael was having none of it. "Bullshit!" he exclaimed and directed his assistant to get the man on the phone.

"He didn't bellow, 'I'll sue you' or come at him in any way like that," Kolber recalls. "It was, 'Look, we both had too much to drink, but you know this is a great opportunity and you don't want to miss out on this. You know I won't let you down.' Something like that. Easy-going, but he damn sure wasn't going to let it go."

As 1985 arrived, so did a $3.5 million loan from the man's company. It was a fine way to start the new year as were other encouraging signs that the blood, sweat, and tears poured into Air Atlanta were paying off.

In late January, Delta at long last signed an interline agreement with Air Atlanta, incorporating the carrier jet service into its computerized ticketing and baggage handling systems. Eastern followed suit in March.

Things were going better than many would have expected for Hartsfield's only specialty carrier, and an airline in its infancy at that. Even the rough spots had been smoothed over. When Brandt quit the previous summer, so had two other top executives – vice presidents Jim Purcell (operations) and Cheung Wong (marketing), who echoed Brandt's complaints about Michael's unseemly involvement in Air Atlanta's operational affairs, in which they were purportedly expert and he allegedly was not. They also didn't like that Michael maintained a plush office at the airport in addition to his small office downtown—an extravagance that couldn't be justified, they said—and they objected to the chairman's habit of flying first class on his airline even though the employee handbook expressly allowed that perk for members of the board.

"I resigned because Rod Brandt resigned," Purcell later told *Atlanta Weekly* magazine. "And it was caused by Michael Hollis deciding to move out [of his downtown office] and reign over the company. I didn't feel it would work. I felt he was jeopardizing the future of the airline."

Then as before, Michael had weathered the resignations with aplomb and with the board's full support, enabling him to move on without controversy. All three men were soon replaced. Airline veteran Neil Effman was tapped to shepherd Air Atlanta into what looked like a promising future. The chemistry was good between Michael and Effman, who took the job after he was unexpectedly passed over for the CEO position at TransWorld Airlines when Charles Meyer retired.

With Effman as president and Michael as CEO and chairman of the board, one-year-old Air Atlanta seemed to be getting its wing strength. By the time it had been flying for eighteen months, the airline had a flawless safety record, fuel costs were under control, five planes were in service and nearly three hundred thousand passengers had traveled on the airline. The skeletal marketing department was still not spending much on print and broadcast advertising, but its courtship of travel agents had begun to pay off. A survey of seven-hundred-and-fifty frequent travelers found that Air Atlanta beat Delta, Eastern, and Republic in ratings for seat width, legroom, food and in-flight service, the foundations of its customer appeal.

Delta was still "top of the mind" for three-fourths of the respondents, but 77 percent of them had flown Air Atlanta more than once, an indication that Michael's airline was gaining traction. At the same time, the airline's four-hundred-and-twenty full-time employees appeared to be happy. Each had received a ten percent pay increase and the company's stock-sharing plan was in the works.

At one point, the pilots and mechanics had considered unionizing, which would have made the company's overhead untenable, but the airline's familial atmosphere, generous benefits, and Michael's congenial response quelled the threat. Rather than turn a cold, foreboding shoulder toward his employees – or turn to an experienced union-busting law firm like Atlanta's Fisher & Phillips – Michael appeared sympathetic and let his workers know he would not oppose their effort. After all, he reminded them, Air Atlanta's seed money had come from a long-time labor organization, NAPFE; without a union's generosity, the airline wouldn't even exist. When the vote was taken, the employees unanimously rejected unionization.

Hitches aside, Air Atlanta's first two years were whirlwinds of celebration. The media's attentiveness and accolades were constant. *The New York Times* published a comprehensive and generally positive article about "Air Atlanta's Buoyant Founder" that captured Michael's unshakeable confidence, stubborn ambition, and talent for parlaying friendships into investments. The *Washington Times* saluted the "flair" with which he launched service to the nation's capital.

The *Wall Street Journal* hailed Air Atlanta as possibly "the best-financed black start-up company ever, with unprecedented institutional support" and quoted the nationally respected and renown Atlanta University economics professor Dr. Edward Irons, who declared that Air Atlanta was "perhaps the single most important economic venture that black Americans have engaged in."

In a move that was bound to please the arts-loving chairman of Air Atlanta, the airline received the 1984 and 1985 Georgia Business in the Arts Award for displaying curated collections by local artists in its airport lounges and supporting local plays, symphonies and art exhibits. To top off the praise-fest, the *Atlanta Journal-Constitution* named Michael one of seventeen "movers and shakers" in business across the Southeast. He was honored as one of the Ten Outstanding Young Americans for 1986 by the United States Jaycees. *Ebony* magazine gifted him with its American Black Achievement Award. And Vice President Bush invited him to the White House once again to congratulate him on his new airline and reiterate his support of Air Atlanta. Meanwhile, the carrier born to serve business was widening its realm of influence.

The addition of Miami to Air Atlanta's flight schedule proved to be a bonanza. It quickly became the airline's most popular destination. Air Atlanta promoted the route by partnering with Avis Rent-A-Car System to offer free one-week car rentals to roundtrip passengers. Tampa; Orlando; Philadelphia; Lewisburg, West Virginia; Washington DC.; New Orleans; and Detroit were later added for the sake of passenger convenience and increasing the all-important load factor – the paid, occupied seats – a major barometer and foreteller of an airline's profitability. Air Atlanta had climbed from a seven percent load factor in its first month of operations to 42 percent paid ridership by mid-1986. Although some industry experts said the airline needed to reach a 60 percent load factor to break even, Michael and Effman insisted that Air Atlanta would begin turning a profit once its load factor reached 50 percent, a mere eight percentage points away.

The big prize in route expansion was New York's LaGuardia, one of the country's busiest crossroads for business travelers. Although Air Atlanta had flown into New York's JKF since its first day of operations, most business travelers preferred LaGuardia because it was much smaller and easier to traverse than Kennedy and, although both airports are in Queens, LaGuardia is closer to Manhattan.

Kensico Associates, a national management consultant firm, had specified LaGuardia in its recommendation that Air Atlanta increase service between Atlanta and New York. Kensico had also suggested improvements at the JFK gates that Air Atlanta shared with its international partner, Pan Am. "Gate 19 at Kennedy, which Air Atlanta uses occasionally, is a slum," groused Kensico's report. Consequently, the two airlines pooled their resources to dress up the JFK gate area, but Air Atlanta was more focused on acquiring landing space at LaGuardia since service there was bound to lure more passengers than any number of cosmetic makeovers at Kennedy. Competition for positions at LaGuardia was fierce; there were four times as many applicants as available new slots. Michael pulled out all the stops in using his high-level connections to force the airport commission's hand. He won four of the slots.

Governor Joe Frank Harris helped inaugurate the Atlanta to LaGuardia schedule, praising Michael "for his excellent leadership and his willingness to take a risk." As boarding began, a recording of the pop hit, "New York, New York" played in the background and airline personnel passed out apples to each passenger.

Unlike LaGuardia, Miami, and other schedule expansions, the addition of a West Virginia destination was neither recommended by industry insiders nor in high demand by Air Atlanta's customers. But, also unlike the others, it came with a check.

CSX, the railroad colossus, owned the luxurious, five-star Greenbrier Resort in White Sulphur Springs and was eager to facilitate flights to the area. Piedmont Airlines had ended its jet service to the nearby airport in Lewisburg two years earlier, leaving the Greenbrier accessible only, and inconveniently, by car or train – unappealing options for high-end patrons, business retreats, and weekend getaways. In return for running flights to Lewisburg from Atlanta and New York five days a week, Air Atlanta collected $5 million from CSX, an investment secured by the airline's choice bargaining chip, the zero coupon convertible bond. The railroad's CEO called it "an attractive venture capital investment, which holds the potential for a high return." Michael acknowledged the "strengthened financial base" that would ensue from the new infusion.

Around that same time, Air Atlanta had begun a program that allowed passengers to enjoy unlimited travel for a flat fee. Under the new Liberty Pass Program, customers could purchase a pass for just under thirteen-hundred dollars that would allow them to fly to any Air Atlanta destination as many times as they wanted to over a six-month period. A later version, Liberty Pass II, offered six months of unrestricted travel in first class for about twenty-four-hundred dollars and in coach for around nineteen-hundred dollars. Liberty I and II, the first of their kind in the airline industry, were goldmines, yielding $13 million in sales.

Indeed, the developments at Air Atlanta were mainly positive and encouraging throughout 1985 and 1986, but there were moments that gave Michael pause. In September 1985, a Midwest Air DC-9 crashed shortly after takeoff in Milwaukee, killing all 27 passengers, the pilot, and the crew. The accident shook Michael and his team because the DC-9 was similar in size and style to the 727s Air Atlanta flew. Moreover, the doomed flight was bound for Hartsfield, where it used Air Atlanta's gates. It was the nearest they had ever come to disaster.

"Michael and I were friends with all of the executives of small start-ups and we saw [Midwest's] CEO Tim Hoeksema get transformed by the crash; it aged him prematurely," Kolber recalled. "It made a big impact on us and drove home even more that we were literally dealing with people's lives. If Michael and our team were to let something fall through the cracks – someone off kilter or some other red flag – we would have no one else to blame but ourselves."

Fortunately, Air Atlanta's emphasis on safety, inspection, and training continued to pay off. The airline had Vic Hughes, considered the leading safety expert in the industry at the time, on its payroll and, upon his recommendation, Air Atlanta's entire fleet was outfitted with color radar, new technology that could detect wind shear, one of the main threats to airborne craft.

"We never forgot the Midwest crash, in case we became too full of ourselves or too clever," Kolber says.

In a speech to the National Business League's national conference in late 1985, Michael spoke deliberately and proudly of the airline that had made him a celebrity in the world of free enterprise. It was a boastful but reflective speech.

"I knew that I could assemble an experienced management team and turn my attention to raising the necessary capital," he said. "And this indeed was my turning point because we formed new partnerships that had never before even been considered. We brought together the largest American insurance companies with the largest black insurance company. We brought together labor capital and management capital. We brought together people who had never been even invited to the same ball, let alone danced together."

Interrupted by applause several times, Michael sounded a bit like a politician who softens the immodest recitation of his own accomplishments with a garnish of noblesse oblige.

"I am committed to building a corporation with a conscience. A corporation that blends its zest for profits with its quest for doing good. My struggle is far from over; it's only just beginning. We will be the most profitable, post-deregulation jet carrier if we continue to do what we're doing and we shall. Our investors have what it takes. They will stay with us because they know, as I do, that there are so many dreams and hopes represented by the symbol of Air Atlanta."

Yet, despite his professed confidence in his investors' faith in him, Michael knew that he would have to re-make the case for additional capital every time he went to the well.

"Whenever we were running out of money and had to go and beg more money, we would just camp out," Kolber said. "We'd go to the people we had to convince – Equitable to not pull the plug; GE to not repossess the planes; Aetna to keep investing."

Around this time, one of Michael's friends, premier Atlanta real estate developer Joel Cowan, introduced Michael to Continental Airlines Chairman and CEO Frank Lorenzo, who had orchestrated the acquisition of Eastern Airlines in late 1985. Eastern had enjoyed a near monopoly on air travel between New York and Florida, but after Lorenzo took over, the airline was dogged by rancorous labor disputes and fury over the chairman's disposal of assets, which he accomplished largely through sales to other airlines. With an eye on growth, Air Atlanta's senior executives campaigned vigorously for acquiring some of Eastern's goods, but Michael and the board of directors decided that the timing was not right.

It might have been a fateful mistake. By the end of 1986, Air Atlanta's long-time benefactors were showing signs of investment fatigue. For once, Equitable hesitated when Michael returned for another injection of cash in late 1986 and Aetna, which had always acknowledged that its investments were aligned with its social responsibility program, announced that it was tapped out. Others also said no for the first time, perhaps because Wall Street had become bored with whatever public relations payoff it got from underwriting a black man's dream enterprise and was ready to move on. If that's the case—and no company would ever publicly admit it—then, current events certainly provided a convenient cover for pulling the plug.

The once-booming U.S. economy had begun to slow down. Analysts were warning that overpriced stocks were due for a correction and the White House budget director reported more sluggish growth than had originally been forecast. Reagan's money man and other economists were predicting a rebound the next year, but many investors saw the tea leaves differently and turned bearish. Manufacturing jobs were disappearing, the trade deficit was high and new construction was depressed. These gathering storm clouds would wreak devastation in October 1987—the stock market crash known as "Black Monday."

The demand for more and more capital, always chronic, was now an acute headache for Michael. With his old sources suddenly on pause mode, he was desperate for new investors. The expense of additional planes and personnel required to accommodate Air Atlanta's expanded flight schedules, plus mounting arrearages in gate fees and vendor payments, beggared relief.

Enter KLM, the standard bearer of the Netherlands. The Dutch government was gradually reducing its shares in the carrier and KLM took advantage of its growing autonomy to begin spreading its wings worldwide. Michael had heard that KLM was looking for a U.S. partner to help feed passengers into its international flights out of JFK. Never one to miss an opportunity, he put in calls to friends who, in turn, connected him to the KLM hierarchy. In late 1986, he was off to Amsterdam.

"Met with people in Holland," he wrote soon afterward in a note to Kolber and Julius. "Quite interested." The KLM connection, he wrote, "is critical."

CHAPTER 12

Michael was almost giddy when he returned from the Dutch capital. His meetings with KLM officials had gone so well that he could already taste sweet success. True to his "camp out" style, he spent most of January 1987 in New York meeting with KLM's people in Manhattan and babysitting a deal he was determined to close—a deal that would pump $20 million into Air Atlanta's coffers if Michael could persuade another investor to match KLM's half.

For that, he would take another stab at Equitable, surmising that the company had been only temporarily reluctant to dip back into its pockets. Things were better now, he reasoned. Wall Street was enjoying a rebound. The Dow Jones Industrial Average had broken two-thousand for the first time and was ripping through old ceilings. Surely that, coupled with KLM's $10 million pledge, would be enough to assuage Equitable's doubts about Air Atlanta's viability, especially since it had already pumped tens of millions into the enterprise. There was no reason to abandon its investment now.

✈ ✈ ✈

As Michael was having breakfast at the Ritz Carlton ahead of another day of deal-making in New York, the doorbell was ringing at his girlfriend's stylish condo in the tony Buckhead section of Atlanta. Michael would have probably been there had he been in town and although he had his hands full with trying to save Air Atlanta, he kept thinking about how nice it would be if his lady were in New York with him. For sure, seeing her would be his top priority when he got back. He was already planning where he would take her out for champagne and a gourmet dinner to celebrate the new deal he was expecting to close with KLM.

Michael really liked this woman. She was beautiful, classically educated, and vivacious and she came from a family that was highly regarded in Atlanta, both socially and politically. More than once, he had remarked to his friend Kent Matlock, a smart, party-loving native Chicagoan who owns a highly successful public relations and marketing firm in Atlanta, that she would make a fine spouse and would be an asset to him should he ever pursue a political career. He had said the same thing to Julius and to Kolber.

The couple frequently dined out with Julius, Jeanne and family friend Johnny Johnson, an official with the Metropolitan Atlanta Rapid Transit Authority. In their estimation, Michael was clearly smitten with his new lady love. They knew he was serious about her when she showed up at the ribbon-cutting for Air Atlanta's first flight to West Virginia and then accompanied Michael on the trip. Michael didn't often mix his business and private lives, so his girlfriend's presence was significant—in effect, their public debut as a couple.

Julius and Jeanne liked Michael's new girlfriend though Julius found her a little naïve and dramatic when she talked about how she was going to take her soon-to-be ex-husband to the bank to avenge his serial affairs and the other indignities he had visited upon her.

"Doesn't she know that guy's tied to the Boston mob?" he whispered when Michael and his date briefly left the dinner table following another diatribe about the woman's collapsing marriage. "She'd better be careful. I don't think she knows who she's dealing with."

With her boyfriend out of town and her best friend asleep in an upstairs guestroom, Lita Sullivan opened her front door that January morning to a man holding a box of long-stemmed roses. Probably thinking the flowers were from Michael, she reached across the threshold to accept them and, as she did, a pop erupted from the delivery man's hand. Instantly, something tore through the box. Startled, Lita backed into her foyer and dropped the box of roses. A second and third pop drilled bullets into her head and she dropped to the floor, mortally wounded.

The murder of Lita McClinton Sullivan stunned both black and white Atlanta. Everyone knew, or knew of, the McClintons. Emory McClinton was a former U.S. Department of Transportation official; Joann McClinton was a respected member of the Georgia Legislature who had worked for Congressman Andy Young along with Julius. The McClintons were part of that elite bunch that sent their children to cotillions and boarding schools, lived in gated communities, drove foreign-made luxury cars and vacationed in Santorini. That such a horror should befall a family like that, or the exclusive Buckhead community, was unthinkable.

Suspicions immediately fell upon Lita's estranged husband, Jim Sullivan, a wiry, red-haired Bostonian who had come to Georgia to help run his uncle's lucrative liquor distributorship in Macon in exchange for part ownership and on the condition that he would be sole heir to the business. After meeting Lita at an Atlanta mall, Sullivan poured on the romance and charm. His wiles may have left Lita swooning, but they failed to impress her parents, her sister and her friends, who were all uneasy about Sullivan's motives. To them, he seemed to be an incurable social climber who saw Lita—and the McClinton name—as his ticket to privilege and respectability in his new home state. He had already revealed how deceitful he could be when he waited until the day before they married to tell Lita that he was a divorced father of four. Still, marry him she did, and Lita, nearly a dozen years younger than Jim, moved with her new husband to Macon in 1976.

Crown Beverages was doing well, but as co-owners, Sullivan and his uncle were not. Their management style and business plans clashed repeatedly and, after a time, Frank Bienart decided the arrangement would no longer work. But just before he officially cut ties with his overbearing nephew, Bienart fell suddenly and mysteriously ill and died. Sullivan had his uncle's body shipped back to Boston and cremated. Now the one and only boss man at Crown, he sold the distributorship a few years later for a reported $5 million.

With his newfound wealth, Sullivan repaired to the rich and sunny playgrounds of Palm Beach, Florida, where he shamelessly tried to claw his way into that wealthy, cloistered society as if his life depended on it. The old-money blue bloods wanted nothing to do with Sullivan at first, but he was determined to impress them, buying a historic oceanfront mansion, cozying up to the arts and architecture crowd, and showing up at every black tie social, charity and political event in town. He apparently came to believe that having an African-American wife, even one as beautiful and cultured as Lita, was an impediment to membership in the WASP-y fold and he began to distance himself from her in his endless pursuit of status in Palm Beach, where he openly and serially cavorted with other women.

Lonely, humiliated and angry, Lita retreated to the tranquility and familiarity of Atlanta and began the process of legally terminating her marriage. Her assassin arrived just hours before a scheduled court hearing to determine the final financial terms of the divorce.

Michael was horrified and panicked by the news, which he learned in a phone calls from Julius and Johnny Johnson. His beloved was dead—murdered by an unknown assailant—and he couldn't wrap his head around how or why it had happened. Who would want to kill Lita? Was she the intended victim or was she just in the way? Could it be that the killer was after him too? Julius tried to calm his frantic brother.

"He was worried that they would find some of his things at Lita's place and he would somehow be implicated," Julius said. "Eldrin Bell said he would assign a top homicide detective to investigate."

Bell was a colorful character who had risen through the Atlanta Police Department ranks from patrolman in 1962 to major at the time of Lita's murder and was in line to become chief. He had been the Hollis' neighbor in the vibrant black West End enclave where many of Atlanta's most notable black citizens resided, including scholar Dr. Vincent Harden, State Representative Julian Bond, civil rights firebrands H. Rap Brown and Stokely Carmichael and Congressman John Lewis. With its all-for-one ethos, the community also produced Dr. Sidney Harris, the first African-American dean of the J. Mack Robinson Graduate School of Business at Georgia State University; and his wife, Dr. Mary Harris, a pioneering geneticist.

Bell was yet another of the father figures and role models who kept the Hollis boys on the straight and narrow. He knew Michael as well as he knew his own children. No one had to convince him that the bright and well-mannered man he had known since boyhood had nothing to do with the tragedy. The Michael he knew had never once been violent, vengeful or out of control. In fact, Michael had never had so much as a school detention. Bell wanted to shield Michael from any unseemly speculation that might ensue from Lita's murder. More importantly, he wanted to protect him from any ties that might peg him as another target for the mysterious and still-at-large killer. Detective Sidney Dorsey worked the case. (Dorsey would later become notorious for his conviction in the murder-for-hire of Derwin Brown, the man who unseated Dorsey in the DeKalb County Sheriff's race of 2000. Dorsey was sentenced to life in prison for the crime.)

When Michael returned to Atlanta, he didn't go home to his comfortable condo at the Landmark. Nor did he bunk at his brother's house or his mother's home, fearing they would be the first places a killer would come looking for him if, in fact, someone was after him too for some reason.

"He stayed in my old room at my parents' house for a few days after Lita was murdered," Kim Alexander revealed. "He was distraught and afraid."

Kim's mother, Janis, had not hesitated when Michael asked if he could hunker down at the house she shared with her second husband, Skip Perkins, whom Janis had married years after the tragic accident that claimed the life of T.M. Alexander, Jr. As with Mr. Alexander, Michael had befriended Skip, allowing his relationship with Janis and her children to comfortably proceed. Michael had always been welcome in Janis' home and that was not about to change even under the mortifying circumstances.

"When Michael came and stayed at the house after Lita was found, he was there for almost a week, just sort of gathering his thoughts," Janis Perkins recalls. "He was sad. He talked about her and his relationship with her. It was such a shock for him that he needed to just regroup. We kind of left him to himself to do that."

Although Jim Sullivan was the prime suspect in his estranged wife's murder, he seemed to be Teflon-coated when it came to making charges stick. When a judge ruled that the evidence against Sullivan was insufficient for trial, the bon vivant slithered off and resumed his stylish life without hesitation. The notoriety of the high-profile case turned him into a pariah in Palm Beach, but Sullivan seemed neither shaken nor stirred. Eight months after the murder, he married a thrice-divorced, Korean-born Palm Beach socialite named Suki Rogers and the couple flitted around the island as if it nothing had happened.

Lita's heartbroken parents refused to give up, however. In 1994, they won a wrongful death lawsuit against their former son-in-law. The jury awarded $4 million to the McClintons, but more than 20 years later, they had yet to collect a dime from Sullivan who, it was suspected, had hidden his millions in foreign accounts. The criminal case was still open, but going nowhere.

Then, in 1998, a North Carolina ne'er-do-well named Phillip Anthony Harwood was arrested after his former girlfriend told investigators that she was present when Sullivan hired Harwood to kill Lita for $25,000. The information comported with what Suki Rogers, since divorced from Sullivan, had told authorities six years earlier. Harwood was charged with murder, but he took a plea deal on the lesser charge of voluntary manslaughter and spilled the beans on Sullivan, who was promptly indicted for murder by a Fulton County Grand Jury.

Lita's family and friends rejoiced that Sullivan was, at last, being brought to justice, but their relief was short-lived. Just when authorities thought they finally had him, Sullivan vanished, beginning what would be three years on the run. Occasional reports of sightings in Costa Rica,

Panama, Guatemala, Venezuela, Ireland and Malaysia yielded nothing. It was not until the case was featured on a worldwide broadcast of "America's Most Wanted" that the conniving fugitive was finally apprehended in Thailand, where he was living comfortably with a Thai girlfriend who had fled Palm Beach with him. Sullivan strenuously fought extradition but was eventually returned to the U.S. to stand trial for felony murder.

In 2006, at age 64, he was convicted and sentenced to life in prison without the possibility of parole, his elaborate lifestyle replaced by the changeless oppression of permanent incarceration.

Michael didn't have another serious relationship until more than a decade after Lita's death.

Throughout the turmoil and grief, Michael managed to keep the KLM deal alive and ripe for the picking, lacking only the matching investment to close. Expecting to get Equitable on board, he eagerly supplied documentation to verify the Dutch airline's commitment. That kind of proof had always been enough to pry hesitant lenders and investors off the fence, so it astonished Michael when his old partners refused to budge.

Momentarily stunned, Michael regrouped then pressed again and again. At last, the executives agreed to put up yet another $10 million to match KLM's ante and Michael exhaled. But there was a catch: he and most of Air Atlanta's board members would have to resign in order for the deal to go forward. Equitable was adamant about it: Either Michael and the others abdicate or no deal.

Even before that devastating blow, there were signs that Air Atlanta's better days were on the wane. In mid-February, Berl Bernhard, the Washington aviation lawyer who had been one of Michael's earliest and most ardent supporters, tendered his resignation "with more personal sadness and hurt than you may ever realize." The resignation came shortly after Air Atlanta's latest chief operating officer, Harry A. Kimbriel, was fired in the wake of ongoing conflicts with Michael over how the airline should be run. Kimbriel, who was Equitable's choice as CEO, was brought in when the affable Neil Effman left Air Atlanta for Pan Am.

"You have always come through in times of crises and I hope you will again," Bernhard wrote. As disappointed as he was by Bernhard's departure, Michael took heart in that hopeful passage.

He had a decidedly different reaction when Maynard Jackson began talking about the airline's future in bleak terms and prodded Michael to consider Equitable's terms. This, after all, was not just a friend and not just a business colleague. This was Maynard, the man Michael had worked for, believed in, counted on, and supported since Jackson's political infancy. Maynard was more kin than colleague and Michael took his apostasy personally.

Adding insult to injury, Air Atlanta's pilots and some of its other employees had started rallying for Michael's ouster, openly campaigning for their founder to quit. One day, Michael and Kolber arrived at Hartsfield to find "Dump Hollis" bumper stickers plastered across the entrance to the dispatch office. The CEO and his vice president took a deep breath and, in silence, began peeling the damning stickers off the doors.

If Michael ever seriously entertained Equitable's ultimatum, even with so many factions arrayed against him, he never let on. His immediate and sustained position was an unequivocal "no" and everything about him—his expressions, statements, tone of voice, body language—showed that he was defiantly opposed to even considering abandoning an enterprise that would not exist had it not been for his imagination and drive. He was insulted by the proposition and felt betrayed by what appeared to be a hostile attempt to take over his brainchild. He was disgusted by the condescension, repulsed by the audacity and sickened by the racist undertones of Equitable's demands. To the world, Michael would present a game face of confidence and resolve, but inside, he was confounded that he had raised more than $80 million to build his airline yet could not find $10 million to save it. He refused to believe that he wouldn't surmount the challenge and continued reaching out to new and far-flung sources, from a multi-millionaire venture capitalist in Washington, D.C., to Julius' connections with the executive chairman of the Hyundai Corporation in Seoul, South Korea.

February brought a ray of hope when E.F. Hutton, the underwriter that had walked away from Air Atlanta's public offering, kicked in $5 million. The investment was the fruit of Bill and Camille Cosby's advocacy. Enlisted by friends of his and Michael's, the comedian used his considerable clout and renown as one of the most popular and influential entertainers in the country to tease the money out of an investor that had jilted the airline three years earlier.

It was a rare bit of good fortune in the early months of 1987 and Michael was encouraged enough in mid-March to write a memo to the Air Atlanta staff whose morale was sinking fast.

I am issuing this communication from New York City. I have been here since March 2, in constant meetings with our investors and investment banker, E. F. Hutton & Co. Efforts are being made to raise additional capital and many of the best minds in the airline industry are involved in our efforts. I am quite pleased and know with certainty that we have the full resources of E. F. Hutton working on our behalf.

I deeply appreciate and understand that you are concerned about our future and are anxious for good news from me. I pledge to you that I will communicate this as soon as possible. I ask for your continued support of each other and the company. I am optimistic that we will see ourselves emerge as a stronger and better-capitalized airline.

Hang tough!

The memo was not enough to slow an exodus by employees who were unwilling to stick around to see if Air Atlanta would recover. Accordingly, operations suffered and customer complaints began mounting, mainly about canceled flights.

"Someone is out to sabotage what's left of this doomed Air Atlanta," one employee tattled to Michael and other top executives in a March 24th memo about a canceled flight from Atlanta to Miami, the airline's most popular route. "The decision was made today…in my opinion, without any consideration for sixty-one desperate passengers, and without first considering other alternatives.

"If there is anyone left in this organization that cares enough to investigate this particular incident caused by people who already have acquired employment elsewhere and couldn't care less whether Air Atlanta flies or not, I think we all will be surprised at some of the alternatives that are available in some of our mechanical situations that almost always result in cancellation."

To make matters worse, ridiculous rumors sprung up around Hartsfield that Air Atlanta's jets were being used to smuggle illegal drugs to and from the cities it served – an abject lie that coincided with the arrest of sixteen current and former Pan Am, Delta and Eastern employees indicted on charges of helping smuggle $1.5 billion of cocaine from Brazil to JFK. Air Atlanta had no ties whatsoever to the drug ring and was never implicated in the illicit operation, which had been going on for six years under the direction of two brothers from The Netherlands. Still, despite their utter fiction, the scandalous rumblings were salt in the wound.

By March 1987, Michael had shifted his hunt for capital into high gear, practically living in New York and going door-to-door on Wall Street, enlisting help from the scores of powerhouse contacts he had amassed over the years, but time was running out. The airline, having already sold one of its planes to Federal Express and its gates and landing slots in Washington, D.C., was in danger of losing its operating privileges at Hartsfield, its home base, where it owed nearly $400,000 in delinquent landing and rental fees. After an emergency meeting with investors in New York, it was able to make a $50,000 payment against the arrearages, but that wouldn't suffice for long. The walls were caving in slowly, surely and sometimes embarrassingly, as in the time Michael Chowdry, head of a Colorado aeronautics leasing company, showed up in the middle of Dan Kolber's interview with *The New York Times* to announce that he had come to repossess his planes. According to the Times story:

> *Mr. Kolber explained that $10 million additional financing was being sought at that moment to allow the airline to pay Mr. Chowdry, lease additional planes and achieve "critical mass."*

> *"What you have here," Mr. Chowdry replied coolly, "is a critical mess."*

As late as March 23, KLM was telling the Reuters news agency that a loan to Air Atlanta was still in the works and that, contrary to speculation, it was not considering a takeover but rather a partnership. But, a week and a half later, it was inarguably clear that if any matching money was coming, it was not coming fast enough. Air Atlanta, Inc., sought Chapter 11 federal bankruptcy protection, a last ditch effort to regroup and survive. The petition argued that Air Atlanta was wounded but alive and needed only relief from the unrelenting pressure of servicing its large and, in some cases, delinquent debts, to restore its health and prosper – a perfunctory argument, to be sure. Air Atlanta was immediately grounded and its employees were laid off.

Unusually, not a single creditor contested Air Atlanta's petition. Nor did a single passenger or employee file a claim.

CHAPTER 13

Despite the bankruptcy filing in the first week of April 1987, Michael spent most of that month trying to revive his failing airline, holding to an exhausting schedule of meetings with potential investors in New York. The KLM deal was still in the pipeline and if any one of the new prospects would match the offer, it was not too late to get the bills caught up, discharge the Chapter 11, and get the planes flying again. There was a lot of catching up to do. Air Atlanta was behind on its rent to the City of Atlanta for the Hartsfield space to the tune of $365,000. It owed $40,000 to Philadelphia for four months of landing fees. It was 30 days behind on its Memphis landing fees. And it was woefully behind on payments for the three planes it leased from two aeronautics companies. GECC had already repossessed Air Atlanta's four original planes. It was just a matter of time before Michael Chowdry reappeared and this time, there was no question that he would not leave without his planes. Michael was hustling against the clock.

But, as Kolber put it, "He ran out of bullets." By the end of April, the handwriting on the wall had turned boldface: Air Atlanta was history.

The last planes were gone, landing rights at many of the major airports had been sold, and the Air Atlanta Board of Directors had voted to forgo reorganization, which had kept the door open for a comeback, and instead, to liquidate. If there was any last, faint flicker of hope, it was extinguished when a KLM official told the *Atlanta Journal*, "We are no longer interested in pursuing an agreement."

There was nothing left for Michael to do other than help maximize the sale of Air Atlanta's remaining assets to satisfy creditors. Or rather, to satisfy the debts. Many of the creditors themselves were angry and implacable as demonstrated in a May 1987 meeting with the bankruptcy trustee that Michael failed to attend. Several of the 150 interested parties at the meeting stormed out when they learned that the last standing official of Air Atlanta would not be there to answer their questions. Some of the 100 former employees there fumed that the meeting had to be rescheduled, meaning it would be just that much longer before they would find out when they could cash their final paychecks—useless pieces of paper as long as Air Atlanta's bank accounts were frozen.

The former staffers also wanted to ask Michael why Air Atlanta had hosted an extravagant $65,000 party at the Fox shortly before the airline filed for bankruptcy. It had been one hell of a party, they concurred. "We had a blast," said one. Still, they wondered why Michael had put on such a spectacle, replete with limos, lights, and champagne, for an airline in extremis.

They would not get answers until July when the Meeting of Creditors took place with Michael in attendance at last. The *Atlanta Journal-Constitution* noted that when Michael strode in, dressed in a "crisp, dark blue suit," he was greeted by both applause—from friends like entertainer Freddy Cole, the youngest brother of legendary songster Nat King Cole—and jeers from unhappy former employees and creditors.

The $65,000 anniversary party, he told them, had been necessary to both lift employee morale and impress investors who might be inspired to pony up more cash. As for when their last paychecks would be viable, that was the bankruptcy trustee's call.

The peeved workers let their former boss know that they were appalled that he was still drawing a $1,500-a-week salary and reimbursing himself for travel expenses. Michael countered that he was working hard to secure the best deals he could get for the company's dwindling assets in order to settle its debts and that "I'm not going to work for nothing."

Michael's style and demeanor at the July meeting struck many of the attendees as arrogant and impassive. Indeed, image consultants might have advised him to adopt an "Everyman" persona when facing impatient men and women he owed money to but was unable to pay. No expensive, custom-made suit, Italian leather shoes, and monogrammed shirts that day. No dispassionate recitation of the facts. And no coldly ironic statements like, "I'm not going to work for nothing" in front of people who had been forced to do just that.

But Michael didn't have image consultants and, given his stubborn independence, might not have heeded them anyway. By nature, he was incapable of a public mea culpa, or of dressing like a workaday stiff, or of bewailing his fate and casting himself as a victim. Or of accepting the role of villain. To him, Air Atlanta's descent was as much a part of the gamble as was its ascendancy. While he felt responsible for what had happened to his former employees and creditors, he did not feel guilty. He had poured his heart and soul into making Air Atlanta happen, had worked tirelessly to build and maintain it, had turned over every rock to rescue it. When things were going well, planes flew, people had good jobs and Air Atlanta was the pride and joy of the black business world and the pride of the industry. Now that all of that was gone, Michael saw no purpose in cursing the fates. For him, matter-of-factness was only appropriate and fair. He was calm because he had come to terms with reality. He dressed smartly because he was still a businessman and believed in looking the part. He was confident because he had faith that he would recover and triumph again. In his mind, Air Atlanta had been a success, just not one that lasted as long as he had hoped. "It was a miracle that we lasted three years," he told a journalist.

One evening in late 1987, a small truck pulled up to the front of Julius' home in the charming neighborhood of Morningside, laden with boxes of documents. Solemnly and silently, Michael began moving the boxes into the house, aided by a trusted protégé, Paxton Baker. This was the last, remaining existential evidence of an airline that no longer flew, the proof of a dream once realized, now vanquished. Entrusting the documents to his brother felt like laying to rest an accomplishment that he would never forget and Michael could not help but shed a few tears. Five days later, the Chapter 11 petition was converted to a Chapter 7 filing, wiping out the airline's future along with its debts. Planes and other vehicles, fuel inventory, landing slots and everything else was sold off under the auspices of the federal bankruptcy trustee. The airline that had defied the odds for three years, living by the seat of its pants, was finished.

"The only people who did not get paid were the Equitable and the Aetnas of the world," Kolber explained. "Robert White, the NAPFE president, had an opponent who went after him, telling everybody, 'He's going to lose our money,' so Michael made provisions to get NAPFE its money back. He appreciated the historical importance of NAPFE's investment in Air Atlanta. There's no reason to give an early investor his money back, but NAPFE got paid. That was number one."

Outside public view, Michael mourned the demise of his foundling and its inglorious end. The layoffs, the hit to his reputation, the disappointing blow to the black community that had been so proud of Air Atlanta, the depletion of so much real and political capital, the residue of "what might have been"—all of it left him profoundly sad.

"Fifteen percent of something was missing," says Kim Alexander, recalling how different her old friend seemed when Air Atlanta closed. She had worked there during her summers off from school and had seen firsthand how energized and determined Michael was. Knowing him so well, she couldn't help but notice the deflation.

"He was down," Julius concedes. "For a minute."

True to form, Michael autopsied the Air Atlanta experience in search of whatever lessons it had to offer so that he could apply them to his next act, which was as certain to happen as the day is long. Many a glass of wine and pitcher of beer were emptied during the series of post-mortems that took place over poker and dinner tables with the men he trusted most— Julius, Kolber, Gary Love, Chuck Williams, Johnny Johnson, Kent Matlock, and Atlanta businessman Frank Monteith. The friends agreed that if there was any one thing that would have made a difference, it was for Air Atlanta to have seized upon the opportunity to take over Eastern Airlines when it was hanging on by a thread. Granted, that move would have catapulted Air Atlanta into the major leagues and eased profit pressures by spreading fixed costs over a larger fleet and higher load factors. But, it also posed calculated risks and would initially ratchet up costs and commitments. Equitable, a big investor also in Eastern, had hinted that it would back such a move, but Michael suspected some serious strings would be attached to that deal. Ultimately, he and the board decided to pass on Eastern for the time being, not knowing it would be their only shot.

Michael also revisited his relationship with the four men he had brought in to run the day-to-day operations, each of whom brought decades of industry expertise to the table. He wished just one of them had commanded his trust and made him comfortable with letting go, but that never happened. Neil Effman had come close, but even with him, Michael believed it was necessary to keep a firm hand on the controls. Quite possibly, he never could have let go completely with anyone, given that no one fully shared his vision of what the airline could be nor did anyone bear the responsibility for things like safety and payrolls like he did.

Michael rued the falling out with his long-time mentor, friend, and collaborator Maynard Jackson, whose push for Michael's abdication in the airline's final days still felt more like a personal betrayal—a no-confidence vote—than merely a tough business call. The two would maintain some business ties for the rest of their lives and would always be cordial to one another, but their relationship would never again be the same.

As summer settled in, Michael and a trio of friends took off for the Montreux Jazz Festival in Switzerland, a hugely popular event second in size only to the yearly musical merrymaking in Montreal. Freddy Cole had introduced him to the annual festival the year before and that foray had hooked Michael, who vowed to become a regular. That July of 1987, he looked forward to Montreux with even more excitement than the first time, both because he knew what good times were in store for him and because he needed a break from the headaches of dissolving Air Atlanta and heartbreaks of having lost both it and Lita in the first four months of the year. He knew that a few hot summer days and cool summer nights on Lake Geneva in the foothills of the Alps with jazz artists to serenade him, friends to humor him, and great food and wine to fuel him would be manna for his weary spirit. Freddy and other well-connected friends would make sure that Michael and his party had backstage access to the major acts and were invited to all of the A-list parties.

At one such gathering, Michael was introduced to Nina Simone, a headliner at Montreux, and he spent several hours chatting and laughing with her, getting cozier as the night grew long. After that, Michael and the famous chartreuse spent several intimate nights together under the Swiss stars.

He returned to Atlanta with his next project already underway. For six years, Michael had kept a coveted business chip in his pocket and the time had come to bring it to light. Since the mid-1970s, the Federal Communications Commission had been under increasing pressure to remedy the miserly number of broadcast licenses across the country held by non-whites. The agency's own examination found that whites owned all but 40 of the 8,500 broadcast licenses in the U.S.—a disgrace the FCC decided to atone for by giving preferential consideration to minority applicants.

Here again, as with its history in commercial aviation, Atlanta provided a touch of hometown lore to inspire Michael. He had grown up listening to disc jockeys and soul music on Atlanta's WERD, the first black-owned radio station in the country and the only place on the local dial to hear music and information targeted to black audiences. When a new 50,000-watt frequency in the Atlanta area became available in 1981, it didn't matter that Michael was too busy exploring the frontiers of airline deregulation to start a radio station. He pounced on the opportunity and filed an application for ownership. According to the FCC, he was the only black person who sought rights to the new signal, promising programming for the black community. Given his credentials and the agency's newfound

commitment to minority licensure, Michael's approval was all but foregone. His new station was assigned "WPBD" as its broadcast call sign at
640 on the AM dial.

With Air Atlanta come and gone, the shelved license had new life
and new appeal in 1987. Although Michael had couched his application in
the requisite terms—he would provide news, entertainment, and information for the black community, he pledged—he understood that his FCC
license would be highly marketable should he decide that the radio business was not for him. A 50,000-watt radio signal can reach hundreds of
miles in all directions, giving the station regional power and making it a
magnet for advertisers in several states. At the time, there was only one station in Atlanta with enough bandwidth to serve all of Atlanta and beyond.
That station, WSB-AM, never catered to black audiences even when it was
a music station and, as the 1980s wound down, it was increasingly moving
toward a news-talk format. For its preferred music and community news,
black Atlanta had to rely on three, low-watt stations on the AM dial with
signals that sometimes were not sustainable across town and which tended
to collapse at sundown.

After winning the license, four years passed before Michael took
another step toward bringing a radio station to life. He got a construction
permit in 1985, just before the license would have expired for lack of activity. To keep it, he successfully sought a series of extensions to bide for time
while he was preoccupied with Air Atlanta.

As the airline began to fold, Michael dusted off the old license and began actively shopping it among established broadcasters. With help from Johnny Johnson, he scouted a stretch of land near an old cemetery in northwest Atlanta that could accommodate a building and the three towers that would be necessary to beam the signal afar. Michael bought the acreage and approached Herman Russell, the black construction magnate, about partnering with him and financing about $2 million of construction, anticipating that once the station was completed, the duo would sell it for a neat profit.

In April 1987, just as Air Atlanta was filing bankruptcy, Michael's Phoenix City Broadcast Ltd., signed an agreement to sell the impending station facility and its broadcast license to Jefferson-Pilot Communications for $5 million. Already owners of lucrative AM and FM sister stations in the Atlanta area, North Carolina-based Jefferson-Pilot planned to move its popular WQXI-AM to the WPBD spot, a change that would boost WQXI's wattage ten-fold. In turn, Jefferson-Pilot would sell WQXI's old, less powerful position to a black broadcast group out of Philadelphia.

With that deal in hand, Phoenix City broke ground on the remote site upon which the Interstate Construction Company, a subsidiary of the H.J. Russell Company, would build the towers and station offices. It went on the air three months later, transmitting pre-taped packages of rhythm and blues for 16 hours a day. There were no disc jockeys or on-air hosts, only an engineer who interrupted the flow once an hour for station identification, as required by the FCC.

The deal with Jefferson-Pilot drew public consternation when it came to light one month after the station began test broadcasting in September 1987. Local activists and black journalists grumbled that Michael had struck a corrupt bargain – obtaining rights in the name of affirmative action, but with plans to turn them over to whites.

"The losers are the people of Atlanta who were to be served by a minority-owned station," the *Atlanta Journal* complained. "They won't get one."

While the newspaper noted that there was nothing illicit about the deal—"The FCC permits the sale of stations once they are built," it stated—it was unforgiving about Michael's alleged duplicity.

"Did he intend to operate the station when he applied for the license, only to change his mind afterward? Or did he plan a fast sale from the start, deluding the FCC and Atlantans into thinking they were getting a black-owned station? Did he try to find blacks who might want to buy the station – in keeping with the FCC's efforts to bolster minority ownership? We don't know because Hollis isn't talking."

Growing more caustic with each paragraph, the editorial charged that the proposed sale would extinguish hopes for black ownership of a major broadcast property in the city. And it put the blame squarely on Michael.

"Last year the FCC abandoned the spirit of the law... It stopped granting license preferences to minorities. And if anyone ever needed a reason why, Michael Hollis has supplied it."

When Michael returned from Switzerland in July, he had more than scolding editorialists or aggrieved citizens with which to contend; Jefferson-Pilot was killing the deal because of the final price tag – $6 million – and was asking Phoenix City to refund its $150,000 down payment. Michael refused, insisting that the original price had increased by $1 million because the station was built to Jefferson-Pilot's specifications and they were costlier than anticipated. He would not return the earnest money.

Jefferson-Pilot sued to unhinge the $150,000, only to be countersued by Michael for tortious (wrongful) interference for allegedly badmouthing him to current and potential lenders.

And it wasn't the only trouble brewing. By chance, Julius was at City Hall awaiting a meeting with City Manager Shirley Franklin when he overheard a young lawyer say that Herman Russell was preparing to call in Michael's construction loan for the radio station. Recognizing the turmoil that could cause, Julius immediately called Michael to warn him of what he had heard, urging his incredulous brother to take it seriously, recalling that Michael insisted Russell was a friend and "would never do anything like that to me."

"I said, 'Look, man, if Herman owed you three million, what would you do?' That was a wake-up call."

The turbulence roiled on until mid-1989 when Phoenix City sold its license and station to Jacor Communications, a politically and socially conservative media corporation based in Cincinnati. Like Jefferson-Pilot, Jacor was looking for a more powerful signal for an existing station. Again, the new deal was met with public outrage. The *Atlanta Journal-Constitution* called it a "shell game" and decried the lost opportunity for black listeners.

"The chance for a 50,000 watter (sic) beaming quality minority journalism, features, sports, local issues and job information to a large audience is gone with the wind," it lamented.

In June of that year, Michael's Phoenix City sold the station to Jacor at the "fire sale" price of $4.1 million. It was $1.9 million less than what Michael said the station was worth, but still enough to pay off Herman Russell and other debts. After that, general counsel and friend Will Robinson said wryly, Michael "put 15 cents in his pocket and went to Hilton Head."

Retiring to his favorite retreat, Michael put the radio ordeal behind him and began contemplating his next move, a glass of wine at his fingertips and the lucent waters of the Atlantic beckoning outside his door. He may have had no money to show for the Jacor deal, but he knew he could carry forth his multi-million-dollar tax losses and use the negative profits to leverage future cash flow, so there was that. For now, he just needed Hilton Head to help him to relax and restore his physical health with bounteous good food, much-needed sleep, and laughter with friends while recovering his business mojo. He spent most of each day on the phone, picking the brains of friendly business moguls and old friends he trusted to render sound advice, keep his confidences, and cheer him on. When possible, his advisers joined him for a day or a weekend at the Hilton Head digs.

While Michael was not a social climber – he loved parties for the fun and frivolity of them, not to ingratiate himself with society columnists – he was a born schmoozer when it came to the power centers of commerce and government. Since he made it his business to acquaint himself with everybody who was anybody, of course he knew Andrew Brimmer, the brilliant Harvard economist who had been the first black member of the powerful Federal Reserve Board. The two had met at a Washington party back when Michael was working with the Three Mile Island Commission. Long after he departed the nation's capital, Michael kept the friendship alive, nourishing it with regular phone calls, martini lunches and occasional notes acknowledging some new development, large or small, personal or professional. As was his wont, Michael decorated the relationship with business goodies like consultancy gigs, board appointments or potentially advantageous introductions.

It was his friend, Joel Cowan, who told Michael that an attractive office building he owned was being placed into receivership with the Resolution Trust Corporation and would be coming onto the market just as Michael was hoping to start a new venture. The Habersham Building was a three-story neoclassical brick and stone structure that skirted the Georgia Institute of Technology campus in Midtown Atlanta. Michael had outgrown his space at the Grant Building in downtown Atlanta, the address on the letterhead of the small law practice he had maintained since leaving Hansell Post a decade earlier. At one time, the building had housed not only Michael's operations but also Maynard Jackson's Atlanta outpost for the Chapman Cutler law firm; "Young Ideas," Andy Young's global non-profit advocacy organization; and Hollis Industries, an umbrella corporation for Julius and Michael's assorted enterprises. The Grant Building had also been home to Air Atlanta's offices during its embryonic stage—back when Michael had only a couple of people working for him. Even after Air Atlanta had acquired commodious space at Hartsfield, Michael maintained a skeletal operation at Grant – people whose work was strictly clerical, like the smart but eccentric young man named Charles Edward Oliver, the company bookkeeper.

Only two years younger than Michael, Charlie Oliver seemed more like someone from a generation behind, showing up as he did from time to time with a shock of purple in his brown hair and wearing clothing that struck traditionalist Michael as kooky. He and Dan snickered about it but decided it was harmless enough, considering that Charlie was a behind-the-scenes staffer and they would not have to worry about explaining his often offbeat appearance to business associates. Besides, Charlie was interesting and pleasant and a good accountant.

A few months after Air Atlanta began flying, Charlie quit his job. Michael didn't know what had become of him until April 1985, almost a year later, when the bespectacled former bookkeeper burst into the news as the newly arrested and charged suspect in a series of felonies – kidnapping, aggravated sodomy, and rape – in DeKalb and Fulton Counties. The *Atlanta Journal-Constitution* reported that authorities considered Oliver to be "a mild-mannered but schizophrenic genius" who had set off on a heinous spree the same month that he quit the Air Atlanta job, assaulting "a perplexing mix of children, career women, college students and teenage boys."

Oliver pleaded guilty but mentally ill and was sentenced to life in prison for the rape of a 13-year-old girl. His parents, both university professors, wept as their son told the court, "I just hope I can get some help so I won't do it again."

Michael and Kolber had a hard time believing that the slight and seemingly harmless young man who passed out payroll checks for them could have committed any crime, let alone such awful ones, but the evidence was solid and Oliver had confessed. They couldn't imagine that he would fare well in prison, but it was not something they were going to fret over. They were just relieved that there had been no closer brush with infamy than Charlie's brief stint as the guy who kept the company books.

The owners of the Habersham Building had put up the stately structure in hopes of kindling a revitalization of the warehouse district that bordered Georgia Tech. But a sluggish stretch in the real estate market had taken a toll on them and they found it necessary to unload the property, offering to deed it over to the university if it would assume the $2.2 million mortgage. Although Georgia Tech was looking for a home for its new School of International Studies, officials deemed the asking price too high and took a pass. They soon reconsidered, but by that time, Michael was in the final stages of negotiations to buy the building and Coca-Cola Corporation was waiting in the wings to put in a bid of its own. With a

$300,000 down payment and a $1.5 million mortgage loan facilitated by Brimmer, a Bank of America board member, Michael took possession of the Marietta Street property and set himself up in an expansive suite modeled after the Oval Office on the building's ground floor. Grandly situated, he promptly renamed the building "Hanover House," in concert with his latest enterprise, a nationwide debt recovery agency he named "Hanover Credit Corporation."

Once again, Michael had stepped into a field that was completely new to him. As ever, he was confident that he could master the ropes of his new field and believed that if he hired the right people, stayed on top of industry developments, kept tabs on his company, and outwitted and outpaced the competition, he could make a fortune.

For sure, it was a lark full of promise. By the early 1990s, debt collection had become an $80 billion industry, with more than six thousand collection companies scattered across the country. Hanover Credit was the only minority-controlled collector with a nationwide reach.

Under Michael's "bullet-proof marketing plan," Hanover focused on unpaid medical bills, debts to Fortune 100 companies, and child support recovery—accounts typically representing thousands or tens of thousands of dollars. Before long, he counted Ford Motor Credit, Mobil Oil, the Chrysler Corporation, Citibank and Grady Health Systems among his clients. He had even taken over collections for GECC, one of his old Air Atlanta lenders, and American Express, with which he had clashed in the closing months of Air Atlanta after officials learned that Amex had withheld some of the proceeds from the airline's Liberty Pass sales. Winning over a formerly beleaguered creditor and a former adversary proved that Michael's charisma, salesmanship, and ability to move past bygones were still intact. He brought in his old college friend, lawyer and investment banker Gary Love, to lead Hanover and a staff of four, which eventually increased to twenty.

Both Julius and Kolber had tried to wave Michael off from the collections industry, believing that the business of going after debtors was beneath him, no matter how impressive the clientele or sophisticated the techniques. Michael rebuffed their protests and busied himself with wooing more high-end clients.

Hanover prospered for a couple of years but ended unhappily when Michael clashed with his processing contractor, Datamax, Inc., over services, billing, and software. Once a storm of charges and counter charges was calmed by the courts, Michael sold Hanover's accounts to another collection company. Not long after that, he sold Hanover House to Georgia Tech, profiting seven figures after tense and protracted negotiations with the school. The building is now home to the Ivan Allen School of Liberal Arts, named for the Georgia Tech alum and former Atlanta mayor who, despite some notable missteps, was generally viewed as progressive for the times. The building houses four schools, the ROTC program, and two media programs. There are no reminders that it was ever anything else. Even the name was changed back to Habersham.

CHAPTER 14

Just as nature abhors a vacuum, so did Michael Hollis. His sales of Hanover Credit Corporation and Hanover House netted him a significant sum that might have tempted him to take it easy for a while had he not been who he was. "Once an entrepreneur, always an entrepreneur," was how he once described himself to a reporter. For Michael, the end of one business only cued the start of another. He needed only to identify another opportunity and he would be back on track with his destiny. Constantly scouring business publications, newspapers and news magazines for developments in an array of industries, he spent hours each day talking to business contacts on the phone or meeting them for long lunches or Happy Hour confabs to hash out possibilities. Some would join him at the Hilton Head getaway to brainstorm in luxury's lap.

"I've never seen anyone put a deal together like Michael," Todd Alexander reminisces. "He was relentless and he understood better than most that if you didn't ask, and I mean ask directly, for what you want, then you have no chance in hell of getting it. I used to watch him put four to five calls in to various people all over the country—each one, in Michael's mind, to play an integral part in getting his deal done. Bankers, lawyers, advisors, you name it; they were all being asked for advice to help him 'close the deal.' He would tell each one of them what he was trying to do and why it was important that they do what he needed. And if it got to the point where someone could not help because they didn't have the authority, he would no doubt ask that person to connect him to whoever did have the authority. This would go on and on and on all day for days and weeks until the deal either closed or it got scrapped."

In late 1996, many of those conversations were about Jesse Jackson's call for a nationwide boycott of Texaco, Inc., to force settlement of a two-year-old racial discrimination lawsuit brought against the oil giant by six African-American employees. The Southern Christian Leadership Conference, founded and headquartered in Atlanta, had joined Jackson's Rainbow Coalition and the NAACP in a pressure campaign against Texaco, using the company's public image concerns to leverage their demand for concessions to black employees, managers and businesses.

"We firmly believe we can avoid a national boycott if Texaco is willing to move expeditiously to address inequities in management, dealerships, and utilization of Black-owned businesses," SCLC President Joseph Lowery wrote Texaco chairman Peter Bijur in a November 1996 letter.

Scalded by bad publicity, fretting a boycott and humiliated by secretly recorded tapes that damned its defense strategy, Texaco settled the case for more than $140 million less than a week after Lowery's letter was written. In addition to the payout, Bijur publicly vowed to institute new policies "that will ensure that discrimination is wiped out wherever it may be." Michael knew what that meant and lurched into action.

Not only was the pump primed for him to get a seat at Texaco's deal table, but as luck would have it, Michael had a well-placed connection to help him get the corporate ear – Julius' friend Jerry Bailey, chief of staff to Texaco's vice chairman. After meeting on a flight to Miami years before when they were both getting their feet wet in the world of big business, Julius and Bailey developed a fast and solid friendship. Since the Hollis brothers made a habit of sharing business contacts with one another, it was only natural that Julius had introduced Michael to the up-and-coming Texaco executive.

"One of the things the company had promised to do was invest $200 million with African-American or other minority-owned businesses," Bailey recalls. "And that's when I got approached by Michael about his possibly being able to engineer the purchase of eighty-five to one hundred service stations."

Owning a service station was not nearly as improbable a venture for an African-American as was starting a commercial airline, but it was still relatively rare. Only 2 percent of the nearly two-hundred-thousand service stations across America at that time were owned by African-Americans. It would be a huge undertaking and by far Michael's priciest adventure since Air Atlanta. The going rate on a single service station in a rural area was around $1.5 million in the late 1990s; $2.5 million for a station in the city.

"There are tanks that have to be lined, certain safety measures put in place to stop leaks, equipment, canopy and land costs," Bailey says. "But Michael had the creativity and the nerve." Confident that Michael was both serious and credible, Bailey followed up Michael's call to Bijur with a bit of face-to-face lobbying.

"It was easy enough for me to speak favorably of him and kind of steer him to the right people who would be able to entertain his inquiries and make sure he got a fair hearing," says Bailey. "This kind of opened the door; then a serious dialogue began."

One year after the Texaco settlement—before the ink was even dry on many of the company's new diversity initiatives—Michael inked a $42 million deal with Wallace Enterprises, one of the region's leading petroleum conglomerates, for thirty-two Texaco and Shell stations across the Atlanta Metroplex, plus three parcels of land on which he planned to build more stations. Now, the man who had acquired expertise in aviation, broadcasting, and debt recovery had become fluent in the lingo of the petroleum business, mastering topics like run rates, pooled margins, dealer tank wagons, and USTs. Michael registered "Blue Sky Petroleum" as the name of his gainful new business. For the senior executive's job, he brought on his half-brother, James Bernard Arnold—"Jay," as they called him—who had spent years in management at Exxon and knew the business first-hand.

Right off the bat, it was evident that Blue Sky was aptly named; Michael and Jay aimed for the heavens. The thirty-two stations were just a start, they announced. They intended to own one hundred and fifty stations within two years.

Furthermore, their properties were not to be grimy places on the side of the road for motorists to fill up the tank, take the kids to the bathroom, and grab an outsized cup of cold soda. Blue Sky built upscale stores on the three empty lots it bought from Wallace, each of them located in high-income neighborhoods. The sites were beautifully landscaped; large, sleek canopies stood guard over the neatly aligned pumps; and inside the all-brick stores, customers could choose from a variety of nutritious smoothies and healthy snacks or they could buy a cup of specialty coffee, freshly ground on the spot. As with Air Atlanta, Michael had detected an unmet craving in the customer base and carved out a niche to satisfy it, turning his service stations into pleasantly appointed refreshment centers for motorists.

Blue Sky performed magnificently. At its height, it had more than 600 employees on its payroll. Gasoline sales volumes were consistently high, and the stores enjoyed a bonanza from the sale of other products, earning a small fortune from peripheral goods. The company grossed $5 million a month from the sale of prepaid calling cards alone.

Naturally, the stations' good fortune was good for Michael's personal fortunes too. As Blue Sky prospered, Michael's lifestyle improved. He moved out of his condo at the Landmark and into a luxurious residential suite that covered half on the 43rd floor of the new Four Seasons Hotel in Midtown Atlanta. From there, he and his guests could survey the city skyline through large-paned windows or from the apartment's spacious, covered balcony. They could cool their feet on smooth marble floors and sway to music that oozed through speakers built into the walls and ceiling. Michael's luxury apartment could have comfortably accommodated a large family, but he liked living there alone, joined by the occasional lady friend who spent anywhere from a few hours to a few months there, depending on how she and Michael were getting along. Old friends gathered there often for poker games and cook-offs with their epicurean friend. Michael loved showing off the place to clients and business associates who enjoyed dinners of duck confit, his favorite, or for daytime luncheon meetings featuring one of Kim Alexander's delicious quiches.

Looking after his darling mother as always, Michael bought a smaller but similarly elegant suite at the Four Seasons for Mrs. Hollis so she too could enjoy the first-class residence with round-the-clock gourmet room service, on-site fitness programs, daily maid service, and a concierge at her beck and call.

For all of the luxuries and conveniences afforded by residency at the Four Seasons, Michael's favorite perk was his easy access to the restaurant's executive chef. He took full and frequent advantage of the elevator that delivered him directly from his large apartment and into the chef's busy workplace.

"Michael would take the elevator into the kitchen and stop and talk with the chef, tasting and testing food," recalls Julius. "He considered himself a gourmand and sometimes he'd offer his own suggestions on a particular dish." If the highly trained, experienced chef had a problem with that, either he never let on or Michael paid it no mind because he continually imposed his ideas on the culinary veteran.

The distinction between want and need seldom got in the way of Michael's penchant for stylish living and his rock-ribbed belief that successful African-Americans deserved the same rewards as their white counterparts. Nor, for that matter, did the difference between receipts and profits. His seventy-two gas stations scattered across twenty-one Georgia counties were raking in the cash, but there was also significant overhead, including vendor contracts for petroleum and other goods and the debt service on the various loans Michael had used to acquire the stations. In some instances, Michael re-tooled the deals to get more time or even more money from the lenders. In other cases, he simply allowed the arrearages to accrue, always mindful that big money is pliable and incurably confident that he could negotiate or earn his way out of any hole. With the company till overflowing, he decided the comfortable cottage house he had long enjoyed in Hilton Head was no longer sufficient and that a more impressive place was not only more befitting his station in life, but would create the right atmosphere in which to cultivate future business deals.

He set his sights on a property in Hilton Head Plantation, a luxurious, private enclave caressing the Intercostal Waterway and Port Royal Sound. There, Michael bought a 14,000-square-foot mansion amid four prized golf courses and a stone's throw from the private beach and marina.

"Michael always had to have the trappings of power," Kolber says. "He knew environment was important when dealing with high-powered people. He would invite these guys to his huge house on Hilton Head and schmooze them."

As an occasional resident of The Palmetto State, Michael made sure to get face time with the local powers-that-be. He had gotten to know Jim Clyburn, a former state human rights commissioner who had won a congressional seat in 1993 and was working his way up the Democratic leadership ladder on Capitol Hill. Congressman Clyburn doesn't represent the portion of the South Carolina Low Country that includes Hilton Head, but he and his family had been spending their Christmases there since the 1970s.

"I knew of Michael a long time before I met him, back when he put together Air Atlanta," says the congressman. "We just met on Hilton Head and became friends. Our families got together periodically and we started sort of coordinating our time on Hilton Head so we could be there around the same time. He was not a golfer and I'm into golf, but he was quite a cook and he and my wife got to be good friends over cooking. He and I became good friends over drinking. He was quite a connoisseur of wine. He never could understand my taste for Jack Daniels."

According to the Democratic stalwart and popular civil rights advocate, his and Michael's bond was cemented by their shared appreciation for what Republican President Richard Nixon had done for black economic empowerment.

"I think Michael had a certain degree of respect for me because I knew a lot about Nixon's black capitalism. It was Richard Nixon who started affirmative action – the Philadelphia Plan that became part of the Nixon administration. We talked about that more than we talked about anything," the congressman recalls. "Michael was in a different political party, but I don't remember ever having any kind of partisan discussion with him. We never had an adversarial discussion. I really believe it had much more to do with his entrepreneurial spirit. Whoever lined up best with that was going to have his heart."

Several times, Clyburn's family spent the day after Christmas with the Hollis clan at the Hollis estate, making for happy times as seductive aromas from Michael's ovens mingled with the music and laughter that wafted through the huge house and grounds. Luxurious and relaxing, the Hilton Head manse was also a regular retreat for Michael's family members, his running buddies and their families, close family friends like the Alexanders, the occasional business or government big-shot, or the foreign dignitary who had come to talk with Michael and Julius about a proposition in the Caribbean or in sub-Saharan Africa.

All was well until lenders and suppliers learned that the Hilton Head property had been purchased with Blue Sky proceeds at the same time they were waiting on delinquent payments. Other creditors pressed Michael to sell the Hilton Head property to pay off his lenders, but he wouldn't hear of it. He argued that the property was a worthy corporate expense since he used it to entertain and curry favor with prospective investors—a brazen but not preposterous defense, given that the Hilton Head property had indeed been the incubator whence many a business deal had been hatched. Still, his creditors were not persuaded.

As Blue Sky fell farther and farther behind on its bill, McLane Company of Temple, Texas, the main grocery and sundries supplier for the gas station stores, successfully sued Michael for breach of contract to the tune of nearly $5 million. Eventually, the lenders foreclosed on the properties, selling off the stations to new operators. In a few cases, Michael had bought more land than needed for a particular station and was able to walk away with excess acreage that he could turn around and sell. But by 2002, Blue Sky Petroleum was done, with little left for Michael to show for it other than tax write-offs. And the Hilton Head compound. He still had that.

Money didn't drive Michael back to the entrepreneurial drawing board after Blue Sky folded; he was in good shape financially for now. It was his insatiable craving for challenge, for mountains to climb and doubters to disprove that would not allow him to take a break or, heaven forbid, self-analyze. Introspection was not his thing. He merely picked a situation apart and plucked out any lessons he might take away in order to do it better the next time. And there was always a next time. For Michael, the American business landscape was a blossoming field of opportunities to be picked at will. It was a matter only of which to pick and when, not whether.

Every now and then, he missed the mark, as in the time Julius returned from a South African trip where he had brokered Pretoria's purchase of aircraft engines from Pratt & Whitney, the Connecticut-based global aerospace manufacturer. Julius had not only closed the deal but had learned about a tempting prospect involving a group of dormant goldmines that had been closed by the government years before. A South African acquaintance named Patrice Motsepe was looking for investors to reopen the mines and he posed the prospect to Julius and Ernie Green, a friend and a senior executive with Lehman Brothers.

"I got back to Atlanta and sat down with Mike," Julius recalls. "I said, 'I want you to put up a third and I'll put up the other two-thirds so we can buy preferred shares in these mines that have been closed up. My instinct tells me this is a great deal.'"

Michael wanted to know what Ernie Green and his colleagues at Lehman had thought of the deal. When Julius reported that they were skeptical, Michael started to lose interest. Julius urged him to reach out to a fellow Dartmouth alum, Harrison Wilson, a prominent lawyer in Richmond. (Wilson's young son, Russell, would grow up to be one of the premier quarterbacks in the National Football League.) Through his law practice, Wilson had familiarized himself with natural resource development in Africa, so his opinion held special value for the Hollis brothers. When Wilson reported that the diamond mine proposition would be, at best, a roll of the dice, that did it for Julius. If three of the most trusted business minds in his circle were cool to the idea, he thought maybe he should take a pass too. Despite his hunches, he reluctantly let go of the deal, a decision he would come to regret. Patrice Motsepe purchased the marginal mines himself the next year. At the time, he was a well-known South African lawyer who owned a company that cleaned mine shafts. After opening the old mines, Motsepe became one of the richest men in Africa with reported net worth of $2.4 billion. The shuttered goldmines turned out to be "a great deal" for sure.

Michael's next business adventure after Blue Sky was actually initiated by Julius, who was every bit the carpe diem practitioner that his younger brother was, albeit with a preference for behind-the-scenes operations. As Maynard Jackson's stint with Chapman Cutler wound down, Julius agreed to help the former mayor in his next venture – assistance that Jackson was bound to appreciate, given that the city's business establishment was still fuming over his affirmative action mandates from nearly two decades before, and was not done punishing him for it. Even after so much time had passed, white Atlanta business leaders still refused to do business with him. In 1990, Maynard partnered with Dan Kolber in running a small investment banking firm and, hoping to expand, sought Julius' help in capitalizing the firm. He even offered to bring Julius into the firm, but Julius turned it down and took on the money hunt for fees only, hoping for another kind of payoff.

"I wanted to accomplish two things," Julius explains, "one of which was to get two proud and strong-willed men, Michael and Maynard, somewhat back on the same page. I also felt strongly that Maynard had sacrificed and done so much in advancing the economic empowerment of

minority-owned businesses nationally, that whatever I could do to facilitate a reliable investment for Jackson Securities would be my pleasure."

Once more, the way was smoothed by the Hollis brothers' perpetual care-
taking of business contacts plus their continuing fortuity. As it happened, one of
Julius' neighbors in the Arlington, Virginia neighborhood where he had maintained a home since his days at the Export-Import Bank was a senior executive
with Wheat First Securities, an established investment firm based in Richmond.
Julius took advantage of the coincidence and worked his magic, securing a $4.5
million loan for Jackson's firm. With that infusion, Jackson Securities began a
prosperous run that would make it a major player in municipal and state bond
financing in Atlanta and elsewhere for the next twenty years.

A master at converting clients into partners, Julius began developing
his own designs for a boutique securities firm. By 2003, he had parlayed his
long-held role as a consultant to J.P. Morgan Chase into a partnership, with the
help of former U.S. Congressman Bill Gray, a member of Chase's board, who
introduced Julius to Chase Chairman and CEO William Harrison. Armed with
market analysis, his expertise as a former Export-Import Bank executive, and
the Hollis smarts, Julius pitched his idea for an investment firm specializing in
financing for municipalities, multinational corporations and emerging governments in the Caribbean, an underserved market with high potential. A year later,
Nevis Securities, LLC, and J.P. Morgan Chase began managing or co-managing
what would ultimately become nearly $5 billion worth of securities underwrit-
ings. Julius was chairman and Michael was vice chair of Nevis, which Julius sold
for a handsome profit as the U.S. economy began souring in 2007.

The Air Atlanta founder and chairman in his office as the airline was preparing to launch.

(From left) Michael with civil rights legend, newly elected city councilman and future congressman John Lewis; Lillian Lewis; U.N. ambassador and incoming Mayor Andy Young; Jean Childs Young; outgoing Mayor Maynard Jackson, and Valerie Jackson.

A Boeing 727-100, one of four in Air Atlanta's original fleet. The planes were retrofitted for passengers' comfort, space and convenience.

The ad for Air Atlanta that appeared in New York, Memphis and Atlanta newspapers.

Michael joins Atlanta Mayor Andrew Young at a news conference about the inaugural flights of Air Atlanta. Other airline and city officials also participated in the session with journalists.

The mayoral proclamation that designated February 1, 1984—the day of the airline's first flight—as "Air Atlanta Day."

Flanked by his mother, Michael shares good reviews of Air Atlanta's first flights with airline executives and staff.

Atlanta's First Lady, Jean Childs Young, blows out the candle on Air Atlanta's first birthday cake as Mayor Andrew Young and Michael look on.

Michael and Atlanta City Councilmen Thomas Cuffie (center) and Morris Finley. Finley authored the city ordinance that codified Mayor Jackson's mandate for 25 percent minority participation in all city contracts.

Michael at the first birthday celebration for Air Atlanta. He told friends and supporters that the Airline was on a strong upward trajectory.

Mayor Young stops to chat with Michael's mother, Mrs. Virginia Hollis, at Air Atlanta's first birthday celebration in Atlanta.

His girlfriend since their days at the University of Virginia, Dr. Gail Bryant (left) was Michael's date at the Air Atlanta birthday celebration. Here, the couple talks with entertainer and friend, Freddy Cole, brother of pop legend Nat King Cole.

Georgia Governor Joe Frank Harris and Michael at the advent of Air Atlanta flights into New York's LaGuardia, a high-demand business destination.

One of many media features about the daring and dashing young founder of Air Atlanta.

(From left) Michael, Virginia, Julius, Jeanne and James Bernard at Julius and Jeanne's June 1986 wedding in North Carolina.

Billionaire investor Warren Buffett honored Michael and the other recipients of the U.S. Jaycees' Ten Outstanding Young Americans (TOYA) awards in 1986. Their admiration was mutual.

Michael at the third birthday party for Air Atlanta. Although the event was celebratory, the airline was struggling to survive.

Michael began dating Atlanta socialite Lita McClinton Sullivan as she was finalizing a divorce from shameless social-climber Jim Sullivan (with Lita on stairs). In January, 1987, Lita was murdered in her Buckhead townhouse (right) by a stranger posing as a floral deliveryman. Nearly 20 years after Lita's murder, Jim Sullivan was convicted of hiring a man to murder his soon-to-be ex-wife.

Johnny Johnson was a member of Michael's "inner circle" – his lifelong group of trusted friends and advisors. Johnson's expertise was in real estate and land development.

The stately Habersham Building, which Michael bought to house his new venture, Hanover Credit. He renamed the building "Hanover House" and later sold it to nearby Georgia Tech University.

Michael enjoying repartee with Jesse Hill, Jr., president of Atlanta Life Insurance Company (second from left), and U.S. Senator Wyche Fowler (fourth from left).

Michael and Dr. Akosua Barthwell Evans, a lawyer and CEO of a strategic management consultant firm in Detroit.

Michael received an honorary doctorate from Atlanta University. His proud mother and former Mayor Maynard Jackson, one of the dignitaries at the day's events, celebrate with him.

In 1997, Michael purchased 32 Atlanta-area gas stations from Wallace Enterprises, Atlanta's oldest independent petroleum retailer. Soon after, Michael announced that his Blue Sky Petroleum Company planned to have 150 stations across Metro Atlanta within a year.

One of the upscale service stations that Blue Sky operated throughout the Atlanta area. This one, on Mansell Road in Alpharetta, Georgia, was built in 1997.

Michael's luxurious "getaway" in exclusive Hilton Head Plantation, South Carolina. He found relaxation there and was able to conceptualize and finalize deals in the peace and quiet at oceanfront.

Julius (left) and Michael present flowers to Atlanta Mayor Shirley Franklin.

Michael with HUD Secretary Alphonso Jackson (center) and Willard Jackson, vice chairman of Ebony.

Michael shares a laugh with (from left) Willard Jackson, Secretary Jackson, and Julius.

Michael purchased two lavish apartments on the 43rd floor of the Four Seasons Hotel, where he frequently entertained business guests and government dignitaries.

Julius (left) and Michael host Jamaican Prime Minister P. J. Patterson (next to Michael) at a gathering at the Four Seasons condo. With them is Charles Matthews.

The mammoth "safety net" known as Grady Health Systems. A "Grady Baby" and a member of the oversight board, Michael was determined to save both the hospital and its charitable mission when Grady was nearing financial ruin. When he became seriously ill, he insisted on getting his care at Grady.

Jeanne and Julius with 104-year-old Leila Williams, the Hollis boys' godmother.

The historic Ebenezer Baptist Church on Auburn Avenue (above), now a major tourist attraction, managed by the U.S. Parks Service. The modern Horizon Sanctuary (below) is the current home of Ebenezer's congregation.

Nearly 1,500 mourners attended the Home-going Service for Michael on June 25, 2012 at Ebenezer. Some of Atlanta's most distinguished business and civic leaders paid tribute to Michael.

Among those who paid tribute to Michael were (top, from left) Dr. Leroy Keith, Jr.; Nancy Boxill, Dan Kolber; (bottom, from left) Dr. Curtis Lewis, State Rep. Pamela Stephenson, and Gary Love.

Atlanta Mayor Kasim Reed (top, at lectern) presents Julius with a memorial resolution from the Atlanta City Council, honoring Michael. Julius delivered a poignant eulogy. "Well done, my brother," he said.

In May 2016, the Atlanta Public Schools approved a school to be named the Michael R. Hollis Innovation Academy. It opened in August 2016.

CHAPTER 15

Michael's arsenal in the hunt for business featured a boundless imagination and vision, remarkable resilience, a proclivity for intense preparation, a powerful sense of self-worth, and a covetable network of professionally successful men and women. His was a fraternity of ambitious, privileged folks who had "made it" in terms of titles, wealth, privilege and access—heroes and heroines of the American Dream; exemplars of the kind of success stories that give America its legend and global allure. This group understood the value of business relationships and the truth of the not-what-you-know-but-who-you-know maxim. Yet, few could match Michael Hollis in working a contact to its maximum potential.

The members of this elite club were necessarily proud and highly competitive, yet they routinely shared tips, names, and numbers among themselves and were forever introducing one acquaintance to another – someone a friend "needed" to know as a potential business associate, partner, investor or, in the very least, a lead to one. Sometimes, the introductions were more guileful than genuine, intended to steer a rival off course or to make him indebted for a return favor. The rule was to never snub an introduction, but part of the game was figuring out why it was offered in the first place.

A viable business relationship was one thing; a personal friendship was quite another. Michael was accustomed to striking solid deals with men he didn't care for personally and some he could tell did not particularly like him. He knew he was not everyone's cup of tea, given his disarming self-confidence; a calm, controlled demeanor that could come across as condescending or patronizing; and a tendency to command any room he was in. But then, personal friendships were not the prime objective of such associations; they were the gravy. When Michael did click with someone, he gifted them with generosity and supportiveness, sophisticated experiences, his boyish prankishness, and a willingness to give them the designer shirt off his back, cufflinks and all, if need be. Alphonso Jackson was one of those friends.

Like Michael, Alphonso was a southern-born Baby Boomer, a man who had come from modest means but who, through wit, work, and fortunate timing, had gotten his hands on the brass ring. Like Michael, he was a lawyer by training but was fascinated by the intricacies of financial and political power. While drawn to the Republican Party because of its pro-business stance, he, like Michael, consorted with Democrats often and easily. Like Michael, Alphonso was self-propelled, accustomed to winning, and expecting to be rewarded handsomely for it. He was also, like Michael, insistent about equal opportunity for African-Americans, beginning with himself.

Considering the many common denominators and their shared upward trajectory, it was inevitable that Michael and Alphonso meet, as they did on one of Alphonso's visits to Mayor Maynard Jackson (of no relation) when the mayor was looking for a director of public safety to succeed his friend and appointee, Reginald Eaves. As head of public safety, Eaves had been a force of nature, reigning over the Atlanta Police Department, doubling the number of African-American officers, demoting or firing abusive cops, and supervising John Inman, who the mayor had reduced to a feckless title-holder. But Mayor Jackson fired Eaves in 1978 after learning of his role in a cheating scandal involving black police officers and promotion exams.

Highly regarded on both sides of the political aisle and hailed as the smart and tough head of public safety in St. Louis, Alphonso Jackson was an attractive prospect for filling the Atlanta vacancy and, by all accounts, Mayor Jackson was intrigued. It was during that exploratory visit to Atlanta that Alphonso was introduced to the fresh-faced Oppenheimer executive who accompanied Mayor Jackson to dinner one night. Alphonso was bowled over by the Michael Hollis' intellect and poise and was amazed by the younger man's swashbuckling resolve to start an airline.

"I didn't understand initially how Michael, with the self-assurance that he had, did not alienate or intimidate people, especially with not only his intelligence but his size," Alphonso Jackson recalls. "I was baffled that he had the audacity to create an airline. I would have never thought about anything of that nature."

Jackson didn't take the Atlanta job, but he kept the connection with Michael and developed a solid friendship with Julius, whom he met through Harold Henderson, an executive with the National Football League who was a perennial guest at Julius' annual Super Bowl parties. Over the years, Michael and Alphonso's friendship took hold as Julius brought them together for business deals, social gatherings and major sports events. Their brotherhood was cemented once each bought a lavish vacation home in Hilton Head in 2004, making them part-time neighbors and casting them onto the same social circuit in their South Carolina sanctuary.

"We laughed and talked all the time we were there; talked brother talk," says Alphonso Jackson. "Michael would cook and we'd sit outside and drink wine. He loved good wine and good food." According to Jackson, he and Michael were well aware that their quality of life far exceeded those of most people, but not only would they not deny themselves the comforts of affluence, they wallowed in them.

"I always told him, 'People try to hide being bourgeoisie, especially black people, but we stretch it because we earned the right,'" Jackson says with a chuckle.

Eight years older than Michael, Alphonso Jackson was right where he needed to be in the early 1970s, when doors that had been shut, if not sealed off, to his father's generation began opening for his. Because education was prized in his household, Alphonso—the youngest of 12 children—earned both a bachelor's degree and a law degree, priming him for the many new opportunities that emerged with a maturing social consciousness in the aftermath of the Civil Rights movement and implementation of the Kerner Commission's sea-changing remedies. Following a teaching stint at the University of Missouri, he was named Director of Public Safety for the City of St. Louis in 1977 and held the post for ten years before leaving to lead the Washington, D.C. Public Housing Authority. In 1989, he returned to his hometown as president and CEO of the Housing Authority of Dallas, where he oversaw the rehabilitation of the city's decrepit, crime-addled, overcrowded housing projects and ushered them through the political turbulence of court-ordered desegregation. In 1998, Alphonso moved into the private sector as president of American Electric Power-Texas, a $13 billion utility he ran from Austin. When Texas Governor George W. Bush won the White House in 2000, Alphonso accepted his friend and former neighbor's appointment as deputy secretary of the U.S. Department of Housing and Urban Development (HUD). And when Mel Martinez resigned the cabinet post to run for the U.S. Senate from Florida, Alphonso Jackson was promptly nominated and unanimously confirmed as the thirteenth secretary of HUD.

The position set him atop a sprawling federal agency with a $35 billion budget and a mission of ensuring access to decent and affordable housing for the American people. Its domain included the more than three thousand public housing authorities that managed and subsidized apartments and houses for low-income, disabled and elderly residents across the U.S. That included the Virgin Islands Housing Authority (VIHA), which controlled tenancy at more than three thousand units on the islands of Saint Thomas and Saint Croix.

✈ ✈ ✈

If you have money, you can enjoy an idyllic life in the U.S. Virgin Islands.

Crystalline Caribbean waters, smooth ribbons of sand, and swaying palm trees encircle each of the three islands that compose the U.S. claim on the Lesser Antilles – Saint John, Saint Croix and the executive capital, Saint Thomas. The thermometer averages seventy-five to ninety degrees Fahrenheit year-round on the islands and there is a languid rhythm that all but demands ease and relaxation. Unsurprisingly, tourism is the region's bread-and-butter industry. Each year, more than two million visitors spend a few days or weeks in the islands. As if they need more enchantment, colorful, landscaped villas and sparkling five-star hotels festoon the coast-lines, fostering a pampered, paradisiacal experience.

In 2005, the U.S. Virgin Islands had more than one-hundred-thou-sand permanent residents, some of them transplants from the continental U.S., Europe, and Asia, but mostly Caribbean natives. A relative few lived as well as the average tourist. A fraction lived better. About 15 percent of them lived in public housing managed by VIHA.

Like most of the public housing stock throughout the U.S., the Virgin Island properties had succumbed to decades of heavy wear and tear and neglect. Many units were dilapidated, residents were continuously dis-gruntled, and energy costs were obscenely high. Julius, who since 1993 had successfully steered his client, Southern Electric International, an affiliate of the Southern Company, toward $325 million worth of acquisitions in

Jamaica and Trinidad, later proposed that Southern acquire the U.S. Virgin Islands Water and Power Authority (WAPA) for $100 million. Southern Electric International›s takeover of WAPA promised to lower the island›s notoriously high electricity costs and, in so doing, make the territory more attractive to businesses in the U.S. mainland. Despite the governor›s support of the sale, approval of the deal fell short by two votes in the Virgin Islands Senate. It was Julius' only setback in all of his dealings in the Caribbean but it provided valuable insight into the politics and power structure in the islands — information that would later prove useful for Michael.

The year before Alphonso Jackson became HUD secretary, the agency had taken over control of VIHA to clean up the books, modernize the facilities and streamline operations. Not unusually, much of the work went to independent contractors. One of the companies HUD hired to help straighten out the mess was Smith Real Estate Services, a twenty-year-old real estate management and consulting firm from Atlanta. The firm's president, Pamela Smith, was a close friend of Julius, who forged a business relationship between her and Michael. Smith hired Michael to handle the Virgin Islands project.

Within a year of Michael's arrival in Saint Thomas, HUD named him executive administrator of VIHA, sealed by a six-month contract for $225,000 plus a $60,000 expense account. It was four times the amount paid to each of his two immediate predecessors, both long-time HUD employees, and as the local press was quick to point out, it was more than what the Virgin Islands governor and the president of the United States earned.

As Michael was settling into his new job on Saint Thomas, Secretary Jackson was delivering a speech in Dallas that would create a firestorm for him and his agency and raise questions about Michael's arrangement with HUD.

In an April 2006 address to the Real Estate Executive Council, a minority real estate organization, Jackson extolled HUD's achievements in increasing the percentage of minority contractors with the agency. Indeed, the percentage of HUD contracts that went to minority-owned firms nearly doubled under Jackson, in keeping with his commitment to equalized opportunity. He encouraged the conference-goers to get their businesses on the HUD's registry of potential contractors so they too could get some of the $1 billion worth of work the agency farms out each year.

"Whether it's HUD or another agency, the opportunities are there," Jackson said. "The most amazing thing I've ever seen is the amount of contracts we give out every day. One contract can make you wealthy."

The *Dallas Business Journal* reported that Jackson ended the speech with "a cautionary tale" about his conversation with an unnamed black advertising executive who had been trying to get a contract with HUD for a decade. The *Journal* published the rest of Jackson's story about the prospective contractor word-for-word.

"He made a heck of a proposal and was on the [General Services Administration] list, so we selected him. He came to see me and thank me for selecting him. Then he said something ... he said, 'I have a problem with your president.' I said, 'What do you mean?' He said, 'I don't like

President Bush.' I thought to myself, 'Brother, you have a disconnect – the president is elected, I was selected. You wouldn't be getting the contract unless I was sitting here. If you have a problem with the president, don't tell the secretary.'

"He didn't get the contract. Why should I reward someone who doesn't like the president, so they can use funds to try to campaign against the president? Logic says they don't get the contract. That's the way I believe."

When word got out about Jackson's remarks, the reaction in Washington was uproarious. Policy and regulatory wonks decried the secretary's self-described intervention as discriminatory, vindictive and possibly illegal. Already on alert for any whiff of misbehavior within an administration that many of them considered to be illegitimate because of the 2000 election fiasco, Democrats on Capitol Hill leaped on the Dallas story, demanding explanations. Some HUD staffers said Jackson had let it be known that he did not believe Bush critics should benefit from Bush administration business deals, but the agency's inspector general reported in September 2006 that "it could not be conclusively determined if Secretary Jackson's views on specific contractors resulted in a stoppage or decline in contract awards received by these contractors."

Despite the findings, some Democrats still called for Jackson's res-ignation and the U.S. Senate scheduled a hearing for the coming spring. Facing a bank of suspicious Democrats, Jackson tried to un-ring the bell, explaining that the story he told in Dallas was a silly little something he had made up. He told the senators that he did not involve himself with HUD's arrangements with vendors, avouching, "I don't touch contracts."

Intrigued by the secretary's stark denial amid growing allegations of favoritism and retaliation, HUD's inspector general, the U.S. Justice Department's Public Integrity Unit, and a federal grand jury began digging into the agency's recent contracting history with an eye out for Jackson's fingerprints. A handful of agreements drew special attention because of the secretary's relationship with the contractors. One was with a construction company owned by William Hairston, a South Carolinian and one of Jackson's golfing buddies. Hairston's company had been hired for rebuilding projects in New Orleans following the calamitous and deadly flooding that ransacked the city in 2005 in the wake of Hurricane Katrina. Investigators also homed in on a $127 million contract with Columbia Residential, which was hired to redevelop New Orleans' St. Bernard housing project. Columbia Residential was owned by Atlanta developer Noel Khalil, a one-time business partner of Jackson's who purportedly owed several thousand dollars to the secretary. A third curious contract was Michael's arrangement to run VIHA.

Not only were all three men Jackson's friends, but Hairston and Michael's six-figure contracts had both circumvented the competitive bidding process. HUD maintained that it didn't have to take bids in those instances because the need for services fit the "unusual and compelling urgency" exception to the bid-letting requirement. Reporters noted that invoking the emergency provision required a contractor to have demonstrable or unique expertise in his or her field and that Michael had no prior experience in housing management. HUD officials countered that Michael had acquired the knowledge and skills he needed during his stint as a VIHA advisor with Smith Real Estate Services.

"We saw him having the necessary management skills to lead the Housing Authority forward," said a HUD spokesman to the *Virgin Islands Daily News.*

Even while smothered in controversy and innuendo, HUD twice renewed Michael's contract between July 2006 and the end of May 2007, when he gave up the job and made way for J. David Reeves, a twenty-year HUD employee whose salary as executive administrator would return to pre-Hollis levels.

When Michael left the agency, federal investigations were still underway. Some black leaders derided the probes as the all-too-familiar harassment of powerful African-Americans, especially those who insisted on and enforced affirmative action policies that gave non-whites a piece of the action.

Nearly a year after Michael left, Secretary Jackson announced his resignation, citing that old Washington standby: that he wanted to spend more time on family and personal affairs. Even then, the investigation continued.

Reported *The New York Times*: "It is the story of a small circle of black businessmen linked by their financial interests in the revitalization of troubled public housing and, in most cases, a shared affinity for conservative politics, and how those connections may have helped force the housing secretary from public office." Jackson's supporters repeated their suspicions that a racially tinged witch hunt was behind the investigations.

"Is there something wrong with trying to make sure African-Americans participate in the contracting program with the American government?" asked Congressman Clyburn, a friend to Jackson, Hairston, and Michael.

"You get an African-American in a position where he can help black folks, and people just don't like it," said the president of the Beaufort County, South Carolina Black Chamber of Commerce to the *Times.*

It was never disputed that, contract or no, prior experience or not, Michael had accomplished much during his two years at the helm of VIHA. More than 300 units had been spruced up and rehabilitated; the blight of abandoned cars littering the properties had been relieved; additional units had been procured; and Michael had negotiated a stunning deal with Ameresco, a Massachusetts-based global energy management firm, that brought energy efficient measures to more than one thousand units and significant savings to residents and government alike. The $6.7 million investment would shave more than $235,000 a year off tenants' electric bills and cut VIHA's water bill by more than $800,000 a year. Importantly for HUD and for local authorities who were eager to resume control of their own public housing, Michael had gotten the agency's disheveled finances in order.

"Almost everyone who worked with him said he was the most meticulous individual, making sure that he documented everything that was done in the Virgin Islands," says Secretary Jackson. "He took over a situation that was awful. The changes that he made for the people of the Virgin Islands Housing Authority were phenomenal."

The VIHA job had been more structured and traditionalist than anything Michael had done since his Oppenheimer days. Although he was given considerable latitude and shown deference as executive administrator, he still reported to someone else. His paycheck came from coffers he did not control. And he was taking care of someone else's investment, not his own. Everyone who knew Michael understood that his work at VIHA would have been only a placeholder even if there had never been any question about the circumstances of his contract.

As always, both Hollis brothers had their antennae up for any new prospects and, once again, the timing of good luck played a role. Julius had accompanied Dr. Anna Oleona Simkins, his mother-in-law, to a dinner hosted by the Museum of Contemporary Art of Miami (MOCA), on whose board Dr. Simkins sat. There, he heard another board member say that her family was thinking of selling its Coca-Cola bottling and distribution operation in the Virgin Islands.

"My immediate thought was that the opportunity had Michael's name written all over it," Julius recalls. "The Virgin Islands had become

Michael's new stomping ground. He had studied the political, social and financial terrain. The possibility just seemed tailor-made for him."

Julius began lining up meetings with representatives of Carlos M. de la Cruz, patriarch of the family that owned the bottling operation in the islands, while Michael met with friends at Banco Popular, one of the largest banks in the islands and a custodian of VIHA's substantial accounts. Once he got the financing in place, Michael needed only the right introductions to the right people at Coca-Cola to ensure that his application was spotless and would not be lost in the pile. He found that in family friend Vicki Palmer, the executive vice president and chief financial administrative officer of Coca-Cola Enterprises, and James B. Williams, a respected SunTrust bank executive who had served as a director of the Coca-Cola Company since 1979. Both helped ensure that Michael's application get proper and priority consideration.

It was one of the few times that Michael's steadfastness, meticulous preparation, and ceaseless networking were for naught. Late in the game, Coca-Cola decided to "refranchise" the Virgin Islands operation. Coca-Cola Enterprises, the largest producer and distributor of Coke products in the world, absorbed the franchise instead.

"Michael had worked the deal as always," says Julius. "But the clock ran out on him this time."

Two years after Alphonso Jackson's resignation, the last of the federal investigations into HUD's contracting practices closed with no charges or indictments against anyone. Alphonso Jackson rejoined the private sector as vice chairman of consumer and community banking at J.P. Morgan Chase.

CHAPTER 16

Throughout his stint in the Virgin Islands, Michael commuted often between Saint Thomas and Atlanta, a nonstop flight of fewer than four hours that allowed him to maintain long-lived business, personal and social connections to his hometown. His presidential hopes had all but faded away, but there were still occasional rumblings about local elected politics—intermittent whispers and nudging from friends and admirers who thought Michael was destined for the mayor's job. He did not dismiss the idea and was certainly flattered when friends and supporters urged him to run, but he sometimes found the prodding annoying when he was too busy with other matters to give a potential candidacy the kind of attention and study it required. Nonetheless, he knew, a regular presence in the bustling Georgia capital was essential if he was ever to embark upon a political career and, besides, he needed it for his own peace of mind. Like many Atlantans, Michael adored his hometown and, despite his adaptability to new environments, he was happiest there.

Dena Freeman had moved into the Four Seasons residence with him. Most of Michael's family kept their distance from her, especially

Julius, who could not fight the nagging sense that the relationship was not mutually beneficial, a feeling only exacerbated by Dena's frequent and prolonged disappearing acts. Many of Michael's close friends accepted that Dena was there for the long haul, given that she had been in Michael's life since 2002. Occasionally, the couple seemed to assert the seriousness of their relationship by doing something together publicly, like host a dinner party in November 2006 to honor Nancy Brinker, a former U.S. ambassador to Hungary and founder of the world-renowned Susan G. Komen Breast Cancer Foundation; and Hala Moddelmog, a rising star in the Atlanta business world who recently had been named the Komen Foundation's president and CEO. Both Michael and Dena's names appeared on the formal invitations.

Named for Brinker's late sister, the Komen Foundation championed a dear cause for Dena whose mother had succumbed to breast cancer and who was herself a breast cancer survivor. Although she was not always around for Michael's big moments, Dena glowed that evening as dozens of carefully selected guests milled about the Four Seasons apartment, dining on an exquisite four-course meal that included seared scallops, braised beef cheeks and chocolate pot de crème.

As his time in the Virgin Islands wound down, Michael stepped up his commutes between Saint Thomas and Atlanta to attend the bi-monthly meetings of the Fulton-DeKalb County Hospital Authority (FDHA) on which he sat. Fulton County Commissioner Nancy Boxill, a long-time acquaintance, had appointed him to the oversight body, knowing that

Michael's sharp mind and get-it-done attitude would be invaluable to a board that was desperate for a way to save its charge, the financially troubled Grady Health System.

Grady was the fifth largest public hospital in the country, home of the area's only Level I trauma center, the state's poison control center, and the number one burn center in all of the Southeast. It was also the treasured first resort for Atlanta's low-income residents, the uninsured and under-insured. Forty percent of Grady's budget was spent on services for people unable to pay and one-third of the eight-hundred-and-eighty-thousand patients it saw every year were Medicaid beneficiaries, meaning the hospital received below-cost reimbursement for its services. For millions of people in Fulton and DeKalb Counties – and sometimes outlying areas – Grady was more than the protector it was credited as being; since 1892, it had made the difference between life and death, between wellbeing and suffering for millions.

"Grady Baby" was a proud claim among countless black Atlantans whose mothers had received respectable care there even when the wards were racially segregated. No matter how life turned out, being born at Grady was considered a strong start and even those who later rose to high stations were proud and boastful about having made their entrances there. As a Grady Baby himself, Michael did not think twice about accepting Boxill's appointment to the unpaid position. The prestige of membership on an important, high-profile, exclusive board was a distinction he relished. His incurable devotion to Grady made it a labor of love.

Michael's appointment to the FDHA in 2007 had come at a grave time for the hospital system. Despite its venerable reputation, widespread popularity and

indubitable utility, the hospital was on its death bed. It had been hemorrhaging money for ten years, and at the time Michael joined the board, Grady was losing $3 million to $8 million every month. To make matters worse, the Bush administration had reduced Grady's federal funding, as it had for all of the nation's thirteen-hundred public hospitals, at a time when health care costs were soaring. As a result, everything suffered. Emergency rooms were choked and crowded. Vital equipment was outdated, malfunctioning or in short supply. With morale tanking, staff shortages plagued the hospital at every level. Sometimes, Grady's crippled record-keeping system was so overwhelmed that bills were lost before they could be sent for payment or reimbursement. Embarrassingly, the hospital was two years behind on its payments to the Emory and Morehouse Schools of Medicine, which supplied most of Grady's doctors. The conventional wisdom was that it would take $300 million to $400 million to pull Grady out of the pit.

In answer to these problems, the hospital's financial consultants, Alvarez & Marsal Holdings LLC, had proposed cost-cutting measures that repulsed the community and left it fearful that Grady would abdicate its role as a charitable institution, the very mission that had made it unique and cherished in the area. Even in the face of demonstrable savings, the FDHA often sided with community advocates and rejected proposals like closing a costly outpatient dialysis clinic for poor patients with kidney disease. Indeed, so many of the firm's recommendations were rebuffed that the consultants publicly declared that Grady's leadership did not have what it takes to save the beleaguered healthcare system.

If the privation of sick and injured fellow citizens was not enough to move the city's powerbrokers, they were certainly shaken by the specter of what closing Grady would mean to private healthcare providers in the area and the adverse effect that overburdened, inadequate facilities would have on the economy.

In April 2007, the Metro Atlanta Chamber of Commerce urgently pulled together a special task force charged with finding a cure for Grady's dire condition. It appointed A.D. "Pete" Correll, the former chairman of Georgia-Pacific Corporation, and Michael B. Russell, the son and successor of construction magnate Herman Russell, to lead the group of prominent business, civic, healthcare and academic leaders on their salvage mission. Right away, community activists accused the Greater Grady Task Force of shilling for privatization and scheming to end the historically charitable practices that had always been a lifeline for financially strapped Atlantans.

As suspected, the task force's first report, released three months after the group was created, recommended that the Grady system be converted into a non-profit entity. It proposed a seventeen-member board to govern the day-to-day operations of a reconfigured Grady, with a few of the trustees to be plucked from the existing FDHA. That arrangement, argued the proponents, would inject efficiencies into the system and would pave the way for business and philanthropic giving to save Grady.

Once the FDHA agreed to consider the plan, African-American and civil rights advocacy groups responded vehemently. Organizers revived the activist watchdog group, Grady Coalition, which had been quiet for several years, and staged protest marches and rallies, castigating the task force's proposal.

"They didn't save Grady, they took it over," stormed state Senator Vincent Fort, a well-known provocateur.

Angry protestors staked out the board's meetings and confronted its members. They went after Correll especially, excoriating him as the epitome of white privilege and indifference—an old, rich white man who was used to getting his way and cared more about profits than people, especially poor black people. The encounters grew so intense that, at one point, Correll complained of death threats and reportedly hired private security guards for himself and his family.

Those black FDHA board members who entertained or supported the proposal were labeled "sell-outs" who were betraying their own. Michael was not one of them. Under normal circumstances, he might have appreciated Correll's practical, unsentimental approach to reversing the hospital's decline, but this was not a normal circumstance—this was Grady—and Michael wholeheartedly believed in its come-one-come-all role. He found camaraderie in two other board members—Chairman Pam Stephenson, a member of the Georgia Legislature; and his lifelong friend and confidante, Frank Monteith—who thought the plan smacked of a take-over. Such a power play would wreak havoc with the health and lives of Atlanta's most vulnerable citizens, they argued.

Michael went to work. He, Stephenson and Monteith came up with an alternative plan to keep Grady in the public domain, supported primarily by the Fulton and DeKalb County treasuries, as it had always been, but with a substantial and timely capital infusion from the private sector to lift the hospital back onto its feet. Michael helped secure commitments from Morgan Keegan & Company and Citigroup to provide $100 million in loans to the hospital in addition to $25 million in emergency allocations from the two county governments. Under the "stabilization plan," the loans would be paid back over a twenty-year span with each county setting aside about $5 million a year for debt service.

"I have the faith, I have the optimism that the counties will be on the side of Grady," Michael said after the FDHA approved the plan, 9-1, in August 2007.

His hopes were dashed, however, when Fulton County turned its nose up at the notion of taking on more red ink. Several members of the county commission, most notably its chairman, insisted that the loan retirement would necessitate property tax increases – a common third rail for politicians but even more so when the U.S. economy was slowing, as it was then. In the end, the two counties could not reach agreement and the stabilization plan died.

Meanwhile, Correll was rounding up support for the privatization scheme, calling upon some of the powerful business captains in his advantaged circle to help him transform Grady into a solvent institution. He took conspicuous delight in announcing a $200 million pledge from the Robert W. Woodruff Foundation, named for the long-time president of Coca-Cola who had been one of the single most powerful men in Atlanta.

Several Atlanta landmarks stand as testament to Woodruff's power and philanthropy, including a center for the arts, a public park, a library, a military academy, a Boy Scout camp, and a number of buildings on the Emory University campus. Each is a memorial to the man who once wielded so much influence over civic affairs in Atlanta, that no sitting mayor dared cross him. Indeed, Mayors Hartsfield and Allen routinely sought his approval before making any major moves. Though comfortable with his power, Woodruff was not a tyrant; he didn't have to be. His clout came with the job of running the world's largest soft drink manufacturer and the largest corporation based in Atlanta. And with his impressive wealth. By reputation, Woodruff expressed his views forthrightly but always in a gentlemanly fashion. Still, his opinion packed a punch. Notably, when much of the white business community was either straddling the fence or flat-out resisting the idea of feting Martin Luther King, Jr., for having won the Nobel Prize for Peace, Woodruff let it be known that he would attend a scheduled black-tie dinner in King's honor. Suddenly, ticket sales began to surge. On that late January evening in 1965, scores of prominent white Atlantans were among the fifteen-hundred people who showed up at the Dinkler Center to honor the hometown Laureate. It was the first time the Who's Who of Black Atlanta and the Who's Who of White Atlanta had come together in public.

For years, Woodruff ran his charitable foundation in semi-anonymity. During his lifetime, it was known as the "Trebor Foundation"—"Trebor" being the reverse spelling of "Robert." Upon his death in 1985, his estate and that of his late wife, Nell, endowed the foundation and its trustees renamed it to unambiguously honor its benefactor. Although some were astonished by how much the foundation was pledging to Grady, few were surprised that the institution named for one of Atlanta's most generous philanthropists had been the first to come to the rescue. The only conditions were that the FDHA had to approve the plan and grant the new entity an irrevocable forty-year contract to run Grady; and the two counties had to continue their customary funding totaling $105 million a year.

By fall, it was evident that no other viable options were in the cards. Federal funds were drying up, the $100 million private loan plan had collapsed, and Grady the usual county government contributions were not enough. Always aware of the ticking clock, Michael knew that converting to a non-profit model was inevitable.

"Michael was absolutely certain that the mission had to say—unconditionally, irrevocably, always—'a safety net facility.' Those were his words because, for him, no matter what, he loved the people of Atlanta," said Pam Stephenson, the only woman on the FDHA board during Michael's tenure.

The task force's proposal to establish the Grady Memorial Hospital Corporation (GMHC) came before the Fulton-DeKalb Hospital Authority for a vote in November 2007. Activists, doctors and ministers demanded a hearing, many of them pleading with the board to reject privatization and preserve Grady's standing as a public servant. "The fight ain't over," Senator Fort said angrily. "If some of us have to go to jail, so be it."

However reluctantly, the Hollis-Stephenson-Monteith triad was prepared to approve the change, but it insisted upon attaching a condition to the resolution: philanthropic promises would not suffice; the reorganization would proceed only if $300 million in private donations, $30 million from the state, and continuing contributions from Fulton and DeKalb Counties were guaranteed in writing.

"Michael, Pam and Frank were like the Three Musketeers," says Dr. Curtis Lewis, the long-time chief medical officer at Grady. "They massaged [the resolution] so that it was as at least palatable for the community. Several things were written in to protect the hospital and the patients. GMHC still has to seek approval for several things from FDHA."

Although community opponents were skeptical that the guarantees would hold, it was the establishment that barked loudest this time. Some Republicans at the state Capitol threatened legislation to force Grady into the new governing structure, regardless of funding guarantees. But shortly after Thanksgiving, the FDHA unanimously approved the resolution to re-make Grady with the guarantee clauses intact.

"It's an important step to give us the opportunity and the time to get all of the various forces and people who want to be a part of Grady to not just show us the money, but give us the money," Michael told reporters. "This resolution permits Grady to not only survive, but thrive."

Controversy and outrage erupted anew when Pete Correll became the leading candidate for chairman of the new nonprofit's board. "We find that absolutely appalling that the name would even be considered," said a member of the activist Grady Coalition. Although dogged, opponents were unsuccessful in thwarting the privatization architect's election as chairman in March 2008. Michael and Pam Stephenson were among the five FDHA members appointed to the new corporate board. The other twelve members represented the elite of Atlanta's business, healthcare and academic worlds. Correll boasted that the advent of the racially mixed new board "puts an end to this nonsense about a white takeover of the Grady Board."

One month later, the Woodruff Foundation made good on its promise with the first installment of its $200 million, four-year gift. Kaiser Permanente, the health care giant, pledged $5 million. SunTrust Banks promised to give $2.5 million and the Marcus Foundation, a health and human services grant maker, contributed $20 million. Immediately, Grady began getting back on its feet, paying overdue bills, purchasing state-of-the-art equipment, and installing a modern electronic records system. In November 2008, the facility passed a surprise inspection and held onto its accreditation.

But there were also casualties along the way. Three of the system's nine community clinics were closed, including the dialysis facility that had previously escaped the chopping block. More than 300 jobs were cut. Over time, the two counties reduced their annual contributions by half. Although protests died down, Correll's declaration about an end to accusations of betrayal and a white takeover was never realized. Mistrust and resentment over both the style and substance of Grady's restructuring linger even now and black officials still find themselves having to explain their consent, even as the hospital enjoys a revival and a string of profitable years.

"That was a risky position to take that you could find a new format for overseeing Grady," says Shirley Franklin, who was in her second term as mayor of Atlanta during Grady's tumultuous makeover. "Michael was key in helping the public understand the value of partnership with the private side."

"You can like the way he voted, you can dislike the way he voted. You could agree with him or you could disagree with him," said former Fulton County Commissioner Boxill. "Michael loved Grady Hospital. And every decision that I knew he made, he made in what he believed to be the best interest of Grady Hospital.... The transition of Grady Hospital from what it was to what it is, a large debt of that goes to Michael Hollis."

CHAPTER 17

As he got older, Michael's lifelong love affair with great food became evident in his increasing girth. At six feet, four inches, he was already taller than average and that, along with a soothing baritone voice, ensured that he stood out practically anywhere he went. By his late forties, he had packed on several extra pounds, making him an even larger presence in any room.

Still, he would not allow any amount of vanity or nutritional fads to interfere with the pleasure he took in eating and making great food. As a kid, he had been entranced by his Dear's creations from the kitchen of the humble but happy little house on Joyce Street. What he learned during those many mornings, afternoons and evenings by his grandmother's side planted the seeds for his precocious venture into baking and selling cakes as a ten-year-old. Though he never had formal training, his access to the chef at the Four Seasons and at other restaurants exposed him to tricks of the trade for seasoning, marinating, braising, roasting and basting, all of which he practiced and perfected over the years, turning ordinary dishes into something spectacular. Like the self-made chef himself, family and friends relished the comestible delights concocted in Michael's gourmet kitchen.

It was inevitable that his two grand passions—food and entrepreneurship—would one day collide. In 2003, Michael attempted to monetize and institutionalize his fondness for cooking through plans for a culinary arts and hospitality management school modeled after the burgeoning Savannah College of Art & Design (SCAD), which opened with seventy-one students in 1979 and had grown to six-thousand enrollees from one-hundred countries at its flagship location and its sister campuses in Atlanta, Hong Kong and Lacoste, France. Noting that the food services industry had high and steady labor demands, the business plan proclaimed a golden opportunity to, at once, make money and provide a public service by preparing would-be cooks, waiters, concierges, managers, event planners, and others for jobs in the thriving hospitality industry. As luck would have it, his friend C. Jack Ellis, the first African-American mayor of predominantly black Macon, Georgia, just happened to have an old Coca-Cola bottling plant on the edge of town that would make a fitting site for the classrooms, kitchens, studios and restaurants Michael envisioned. Coca-Cola had donated the building and land to the city and Ellis was confident that he could pry a favorable lease from his city council, since its members, like their counterparts everywhere, were eager for business expansion and the economic windfalls that come with it.

Encouraged by Ellis and the city's $1 million industrial renovation allotment to encourage enterprises like his, Michael drew up a smart and comprehensive business plan for "the MACE Institute," which the plan said was "conceived" by Michael and Dena Freeman. It was the first time he had officially involved his long-time girlfriend in a business venture and Julius, for one, was befuddled by it. There was nothing in Dena Freeman's past that he knew of to commend her as a culinary and hospitality entrepreneur. Granted, she was a known stickler about diet and nutrition, but she was nobody's expert and, besides, Michael had already lined up award-winning chef Joel Attunes, the eponymous owner of a French restaurant in Atlanta, as advisor to the culinary program. Julius worried that Dena had gotten her hooks in to Michael deeper than he had suspected. But what could he do about it?

The elaborate plans for the MACE Institute called for a large, modern facility incorporating classrooms, a production kitchen, an auditorium, a teaching restaurant open to the public, a gourmet market, a small "upscale" hotel and wellness center, and administrative offices. It anticipated a January 2005 launch with forty students; one-hundred-and-ten by the end of the first year, and seven-thousand by 2013.

As the crowning glory, Michael projected a $500 million boost to the regional economy during the first five years of the school's operation. Construction alone would create one-hundred jobs, and when all was said and done, MACE would produce fifteen-hundred permanent jobs and become a "catalyst for new restaurant starts, new housing, and improved quality of life in all of Macon and Middle Georgia."

In Mayor Ellis' eyes, MACE was a winning proposition. "Michael had invested quite a bit of time and money and it was a beautiful plan," he says. "He was a very detail-oriented person; he wasn't a fly-by-the-seat-of-the-pants guy. If he said he could do something, he'd do it."

The City Council was all ears when Ellis brought the proposal up for discussion. Gradually, however, council members began voicing reservations or, in some cases, out-and-out opposition to the idea. When the council voted down the motion to grant MACE a long-term lease and the million dollars for renovation, Ellis was perplexed. At first.

Ellis believes white business leaders and their minions on the council had nefarious motives for opposing the plan. "They thought there was something in it for me – that I brought this Negro down from Atlanta to start this school so I must be getting something out of it," he says.

He also believes envy played a role.

"I realized my mistake," says the former mayor. "You know you have to discuss these things with the City Council and it got publicized. I think somebody wanted to take that idea and do it themselves; I'm sure that's what they did.""

Indeed, a few short years after the MACE Institute failed to win the council's approval, a hospitality training school opened in Macon that bore striking resemblances to Michael's vision.

"It was almost verbatim the plan that Michael had put in place. They even had a teaching restaurant," Ellis says. "I've never set foot in the restaurant. That's my private protest."

The collapse of the Macon deal did nothing to dampen Michael's fascination with culinary arts. Cooking was his sport and he could be fiercely competitive at it, challenging friends to best his knife skills, his creativity with herbs and spices, and his mastery of extravagant recipes. Congressman Clyburn recalls numerous lively cooking contests between his wife, Emily, and Michael at one or the other's home in Hilton Head. Janis Perkins had several kitchen showdowns with him too.

"He thought he was the greatest chef," she laughs. "And I didn't think I was so bad either. So we had these cook-offs – a lot of fun together on many occasions."

Another regular culinary rival was Gary Love, Michael's occasional business associate and old friend from Dartmouth. Although Michael usually insisted on doing the honors whenever Love came to visit from the west coast, Gary was proud to don the chef's apron one night during a visit to Atlanta in March 2010. The result was one of Michael's favorite dishes – roasted chicken with rosemary and thyme.

"Some time after we had finished eating, he complained that his stomach was upset," Love recalls. "After a while, he said, 'Love, what did you put in that food, man?' That was when it all started."

Over the next couple of weeks, Michael had repeated bouts of intestinal gripes, which he treated with antacids, warm compresses, hot teas and other over-the-counter remedies. Unrelieved, he finally took himself to the doctor, who determined that his patient was suffering from acute indigestion and prescribed a regimen of medicines and dietary changes.

The diagnosis and new treatment plan promised as much psychological comfort to Michael as it did physical relief. He was far too busy to be sidelined by a grumpy stomach or any other illness for that matter and was eager to get rid of the nuisance so he could carry on with his occupational routines. But the pain, burning and pressure in his belly persisted and none of the doctors that Michael consulted in the ensuing months was able to put an end to his suffering.

After months of watching her brother-in-law's hits and misses at pinpointing the cause and remedy for his illness, Jeanne stepped in to help direct Michael's diagnostic care. She was already nursing her own mother through gastrointestinal maladies and knew that they were nothing to dicker with. The lovely Anna Simkins was suffering from cancer of the pancreas and her treatment was in the hands of some of the country's top specialists, whose brilliance and bedside manner Jeanne had come to respect. She knew the kinds of tests that would get to the bottom of Michael's condition and he welcomed her help.

Michael had always liked and trusted Jeanne. From the start, he was taken with the bright young lawyer who had captured his brother's heart nearly 30 years earlier at one of George and Pearl Dalley's dinner parties in Washington. Jeanne was Michael's kind of person—beautiful, intelligent and cultured—and Michael enjoyed talking shop with her as a fellow member of the bar. When Jeanne was about to launch a business of her own, Michael had no reservation about helping.

"His business plans were like works of art; I mean, immaculate," Jeanne beams. "He would take what I had done and punch it up—more elaboration and extrapolation. He'd ask me, 'Don't you know how to navigate along the shorelines until you find a safe landing dock?' And then he would research whoever was going to be in the meeting so we'd know how to get to them. It worked too. I came away with the money after the first meeting."

Michael also had an affinity for his sister-in-law's family, a long lineage of educated, distinguished men and women who had used their privilege and talent to promote black excellence and civil rights throughout the Carolinas and in Texas, leaving marks on history that are evident to this day.

Jeanne's great-grandparents were founders of what became Winston-Salem State University in North Carolina. Her mother's father, Jasper Alston Atkins, was the first black editor of the *Yale Law Journal* and the first African-American law student elected to the Order of the Coif honor society, where membership is reserved for those who graduate in the top ten percent of their class. Later, Atkins argued a landmark Texas voting rights case before the U.S. Supreme Court. Her mother was a distinguished university professor at the University of North Carolina. And that was just one branch of Jeanne's family tree.

One of her paternal great aunts, the inimitable Modjeska Monteith Simkins, is known as the "matriarch of civil rights activists" in South Carolina, where she championed reforms in healthcare and education in the first half of the Twentieth Century. Jeanne's paternal grandparents—a dentist and an educator—were esteemed community leaders. Her father, Dr. George Simkins, was a prominent dentist whose movement exploits resulted in the desegregation of public golf courses, hospitals, and banks in Greensboro, North Carolina. He was also president of the Greensboro NAACP for more than thirty years.

Since Michael had always been drawn to men of action and those who demanded and negotiated equal opportunity for African-Americans, he was an instant fan of Jeanne's father. Over the years, the two men developed a warm and hearty affection for one another. At family get-togethers, they could often be overheard pontificating about current events, debating business and politics and homing in on the humor or absurdity of practically everything else. Their shared fondness for harmless mischief raised its head repeatedly, most memorably when the NFL Super Bowl came to Atlanta.

Julius was hosting another of his annual Super Bowl parties in honor of Harold Henderson, who by then had ascended to the executive vice presidency and chairmanship of the NFL Management Council. As usual, hundreds of prominent business, community, entertainment and political stars came out. Though the parties were expensive affairs, Michael and Julius considered them loss-leaders; the networking, accessibility, and potential deals that would accrue from such gatherings—not to mention prized Super Bowl tickets—were well worth the investment.

In the 1994 contest between the Dallas Cowboys and Buffalo Bills, most of the country watched the game on TV, but Michael and Dr. Simkins took it in live and in-the-flesh at the Georgia Dome. During one lull in the action, as the television cameras panned the sidelines, Jeanne shot up in her seat.

"Wait, a minute!" she exclaimed. "Is that Daddy and Michael on the sidelines?"

Indeed, it was. Smooth-talking Michael had collared a field official and asked him if his companion, whom he described as a high-level dignitary, might be allowed to see a part of the game from the field. The camera shot that sent Jeanne bolting upright had captured Michael standing near the players and coaches with her handsome, distinguished father who, as Jeanne later learned, had been introduced to game officials as "the personal physician to Muhammed Ali."

Whether it was ever openly acknowledged or not, Dr. Simkins was part of that special troop of elder statesmen Michael had adopted as surrogate dads—wise, accomplished, thoughtful, generous men like Dr. Harvey Smith, Dr. Benjamin Mays, and Atlanta civic leader John Cox. When Dr. Simkins died in 2001, Michael was one of the pallbearers at his funeral. Jeanne says he cried like a baby.

Six months had passed since the evening that Michael felt that first disturbance in his midsection after dinner with Gary Love. Since then, the discomfort had only worsened. By late summer 2010, he had practically lost count of the number of tests he had undergone in consulting one physician after another within the Emory health system, seeking a solution to his gnawing condition.

"He had been having so many pains," says Julius. "There was such pain in his side that he had to sleep sitting up, he couldn't lie down."

In September, Michael subjected himself to the battery of intensive and sophisticated tests that Jeanne had recommended. She accompanied him to the doctor one early autumn day to hear the results.

"The doctor was just cold and to the point, as if he were talking about the weather forecast," Jeanne says dolefully. "He walked in and said, 'The cancer is in the pancreas and has metastasized to the liver. You probably don't have six months; more like three to four months.' It was that brutal."

Wracked by grief and shock over the devastating news about his brother's health, Julius railed against the doctors who had, for months, misread Michael's condition. He was furious that so much precious time had been lost—months that might have been spent combatting the rampaging cancer cells rather than giving them more leeway.

"Not indigestion, not irritated bowel syndrome, not duodenal ulcers or any of the other stuff they had been telling us," Julius says, the disgust still clear in his voice. "It was pancreatic cancer. Stage Three pancreatic cancer."

The dread diagnosis floored the usually unflappable patient. For a few days, he was despondent and reflective, struggling to come to terms with the doctor's dispassionate verdict. He, Julius, Jeanne and Gary Love came together to form a plan of action. They knew the first order of business was to find another doctor—one who knew how to balance know-how and candor with at least a modicum of compassion. Michael emerged determined to put up the fight of his life in the fight for his life and seemed confident that he would survive the deadly disease.

As far as the family was concerned, Michael was going to get the best of medical advice and attention and for them, that meant only two possible sources – either M.D. Anderson, the famed cancer research and treatment center in Houston, or the renowned Johns Hopkins in Baltimore, where Anna Simkins was receiving state-of-the-art care. They offered to set Michael up in a comfortable apartment in either city so that he could see his doctors and take his treatments conveniently.

Michael agreed to visit both prestigious hospitals and meet with physicians there, but when it came to treating the cancer, he insisted that only Atlanta's Grady or Emory Hospitals would do. Julius and Jeanne tried repeatedly to convince Michael that he should seek care from the country's most reputable cancer hospitals, reminding him that, despite their outstanding reputations in other areas, neither Grady nor Emory was famous for its pancreatic cancer protocols.

Michael immediately set out to meet with oncologists at Anderson and Hopkins, with Gary Love as his traveling companion. They visited M.D. Anderson, Johns Hopkins and other renowned research hospitals, including the Mayo Clinic, collecting ideas and treatment regimens along the way. While impressed by the expertise offered at those venerated institutions, Michael was not always satisfied with what he learned.

"He and I went to Hopkins together looking for a study that might fit his case," Love says. "The doctor suggested that patients in his group had, at best, six months. Well, that was not going to work for Michael."

He was more empathic than ever that only Grady or Emory would be allowed to treat him. Alone with Michael one evening on the balcony of the Four Seasons condo, Julius tried to move his brother off his stubborn perch. He reminded him of many racial disparity studies with their disturbing findings of neglect and unequal care of black and brown patients at hospitals in the South and nationwide.

But Michael was unmoved.

"You're being naïve," Julius said in frustration.

It certainly wasn't the first time that Michael had eschewed the experts and insisted on being the final arbiter of his interests. That's what he had done with Air Atlanta – refusing to relinquish control and dismissing advice on how to run things. Friends and family soon resigned themselves to the decision and hoped for the best.

"I heard about it right away," recalls former Atlanta Mayor Shirley Franklin, who says she believed that "if anyone can beat this, Michael can beat this. He has the emotional, spiritual and intellectual capacity to beat it. We were all hopeful."

Even though Michael understood that his was an incurable form of cancer—even though he was informed that only 10 percent of patients are alive two years after a definitive diagnosis—he seemed to genuinely believe that he could, and would, outsmart the disease. Says Gary, "When he was told there would be no cure, the strategy and our theory was for it to be treated successfully as a chronic disease." Michael chose to look at his condition as a pernicious, painful, and grievous disturbance, but one he could survive if he attacked it with aggression and inventiveness. Judging from the statistics, it was an unrealistic way to view his prospects. But, no one doubted that Michael wholeheartedly believed it.

"In lots of pain, but will get through all of this," he said in an October 2010 email to old friend Dan Kolber. Such optimistic—and understated—expressions were typical at the outset, friends say.

Armed with the information curated from Anderson, Hopkins, and Mayo, Michael arranged his customized care in Atlanta. He would undergo chemotherapy at Emory and receive other treatments like blood transfusions and intestinal stent implants at Grady.

"He used Grady in a way that a lot of people who had his resources would not," says Dr. Curtis Lewis, coordinator of Michael's care at Grady. "He walked the walk. He really felt strongly about Grady, its role. And it wasn't just for others. He put himself and his family in the system that he believed in."

Michael was not only comfortable at Grady, he was in command there, dispatching technicians, directing nurses and quizzing doctors from his large private suite on the third floor.

"Six months after the diagnosis, if you didn't know he was sick, you couldn't tell," says Dr. Lewis. "He lost a lot of weight. And I remember one time he lost some hair from the chemo, but he was jovial, present and cognitively intact."

Between hospital visits, Michael frequently took business meetings and phone calls and was present whenever the Grady board convened. Friends found him always immaculately dressed; still talkative and assertive; still brimming with ideas, angles, strategies; and still on the lookout for the next big thing.

"He was concerned about not giving off an aura of weakness," Dr. Lewis recalls. "Sometimes, he would come to a board meeting and when there were breaks, he would ask to come to my office instead of milling around. He was rather discreet about his illness."

Michael also spent as much time as he could with his mother, Virginia, who moved into the Budd Terrace nursing home after a series of strokes. Given his own weakened state, Michael took comfort in knowing that his tender-hearted sister, Elaine, was a constant presence at the nursing home, leaving only for short errands or to run home and cook dinner for her mother.

"I still have my alarm set for 4:30 in the afternoon," she says. "That's the time I would get back to Mama if I was away."

Though weakened by the disease and the powerful cancer-fighting substances coursing through his body, Michael still could not resist the lure of business, the thrill of putting together a deal, the satisfaction of making the impossible happen.

It was not enough to share his sympathies and advice when he learned that Atlanta's second-largest black-owned bank was on the brink of collapse; Michael felt compelled to do something tangible and curative, something that would reverse the bank's impending doom. After all, founder George Andrews had been his friend since their school days at Washington High and the Capital City Bank and Trust Andrews had founded was a success story that made all of Atlanta proud.

Capital City had opened in Atlanta in 1994 with $300 million in assets and soon had branches in Albany, Savannah, Stone Mountain, Columbus, Macon, and Augusta. The bank had thrived until the housing bubble burst in 2007, burying financial institutions across the country under a mountain of mortgage defaults. Like most of the twenty-eight black-owned banks in the country at the time, Capital City was deemed ineligible for participation in the Troubled Asset Relief Program (TARP)— the $700 billion federal fund for bailing out the nation's plagued banks and thrifts, especially those that were "too big to fail."

Fortunately, Capital City had a TARP-like lifeline of its own, courtesy of Julius' hard work and connections. He had arranged an Atlanta meeting between Andrews and Houston petroleum magnate Kase Lawal, who was keenly interested in acquiring Capital City. Lawal certainly had the money. His company, CAMAC, was generating over $2 billion a year.

But Andrews was not interested in surrendering control of the bank he had founded. Sensing the lukewarm reception, Lawal withdrew his interest.

"Michael was pretty sick at this time, but he said to me, 'Man, we've got to save George.' He was just insistent about it," Julius remembers. Reluctantly, he agreed to help George once again. "We both kicked into high gear."

Julius approached the formidable Sam Nunn, the former U.S. senator and lead director on the board of General Electric, seeking a $20 million investment from G.E. Capital. For a time, it looked like a done deal.

"We got all the way to the end, then GE's outside counsel nixed the deal because Capital City Bank was under a FDIC consent decree at the same time GE was attempting to renew its industrial banking license in the State of Utah," Julius says.

Michael put in phone calls and face time at three major banks in Atlanta – SunTrust, Regions, and Fifth Third Bank—unleashing his well-honed skills of persuasion. Even from his sick bed, he was able to put together about $4 million. Meanwhile, thousands of private investments trickled into Capital City, some for as much as $100,000, some for as little as a C-note.

Notwithstanding their energized efforts to save the bank, Andrews and his supporters fell far short of what was needed to reach the comfort zone. The handwriting on the wall was ominous. For the bank and for Michael too.

CHAPTER 18

As 2012 dawned, more than a year had passed since Michael's diagnosis. He had already outlasted the projected and statistical survival rates, but there were no signs that the cancer was in remission. Notwithstanding his fierce resolve that the disease would do no worse than make him weak and miserable, it continued its terrible advance. Sapped of energy and often sickened by the repeated treatments, he was unable to work like he used to; unable to pursue or develop any of the many business ideas that still danced in his head. With money short, he had become reliant on the generosity of friends and family, including Julius who extended a series of six-figure personal loans to his brother.

With great reluctance and delay, Michael had given up the luxurious condo at the Four Seasons and had moved with Dena to a small house in Douglasville, a small town about twenty-five miles west of Atlanta. The home they shared was near that of Michael's cousin, Victor Thomas, who took on the role of caretaker and valet for his ailing kin. Michael's visits to the hospital had become more frequent and he could no longer drive himself into the city when Dena was away, as she often was. The family was never sure where Dena was off to – her hometown of Chicago, presumably. All they knew was that she was gone a lot, so Victor's assistance was a godsend.

Michael was no longer able to hide the physical toll the cancer was taking. He had lost so much weight that he looked gaunt and feeble. However, his mental capacities were unaffected except for those times when heavy painkillers put him in a fog. Yet, even then, he could pretty much hold his own.

Selling the Hilton Head mansion had not been an option in resolving Michael's mounting financial woes. It was titled in the name of a company he had incorporated in partnership with a Georgia accountant named Dale Young, who took out a multi-million-dollar life insurance policy on Michael to indemnify the investment. Dan Kolber recalls that Michael was impressed by Young, calling him a "very sharp operator" who had his own mutual fund. In addition to a passion for business, Michael and Young shared an extraordinary devotion to their mothers.

The deed arrangement had protected the Hilton Head estate from a grab by creditors when Blue Sky Petroleum went under, but it also meant that Michael could not unilaterally sell off the estate when he desperately needed the money. Besides, Michael had long argued, he would need the deluxe digs to entertain and impress investors and other influential people in his business dealings, which he planned to resume once he got better.

"Michael kind of had an obsession with real estate," Jeanne recalls. "Once he bought something, he would never want to sell it. As bright as he was, he could not be reasoned with about that."

When Michael first started having money problems, Julius several times offered to buy some of Michael's properties including the Hilton Head mansion, which he proposed leasing back to him. But Michael turned down each of those offers after conferring with Dena, who lived in one of the Hilton Head homes.

Whether a function of arrogance, denial, bountiful optimism or their confluence, Michael, though quite ill, still behaved like a man fully expecting to make a comeback and the anticipation of getting back on his feet seemed to bolster a certain frankness and directness in seeking help. Sometimes his desperate straits even led him to take unwise risks. Upon James Bernard's death in 2009, Michael became the trustee of commercial property owned by his half-brother and former Blue Sky business associate. According to a lawsuit filed by James Bernard's widow, Michael used the property to leverage loans and cash-outs for himself. Michael explained that he had lost the property in legitimate, albeit failed, efforts to make money—a claim vigorously defended by James Bernard's two adult daughters, who insisted that their uncle was trying to make money for them. Nevertheless, Roslyn Harper Arnold won the suit against her brother-in-law, who was ordered to pay a $350,000 judgment.

As soon as he got off the phone, Dan Kolber ran to his computer and pulled up Google Maps. He wasn't sure how long a drive it was from Atlanta to Douglasville, but he knew he would have to get going soon. It was a twenty-two-mile distance, according to Google, but factoring in Atlanta's notorious traffic congestion, Dan figured he was looking at an hour, maybe more.

That had been Dena on the phone, asking Dan to accompany her and Michael to the Douglas County Courthouse, where they would be married that afternoon. Startled by the news, Dan nonetheless promised to drop everything and head their way. It was already nearly noon and who knows how long a judge might be available, he thought; did Dena know? When she told him that she had not inquired, Dan suggested that she call the county probate office to make sure they could get a quick marriage license and that someone would be on hand to officiate. "Let them know you're coming," he instructed.

As he barreled westward on I-20, Dan rummaged through memories and past conversations for some forgotten or overlooked clue that this was coming. Of course he knew that Michael and Dena were in a long-term relationship. Of course he knew that they had lived together at the Four Seasons and had moved together from there to a modest house in Douglasville.

But Michael was 58 years old, seriously and conspicuously ill, drained and sickened by chemotherapy and other regimens he had to endure to stave off the devilish cancer. Why, Dan wondered, would his lifelong bachelor-friend decide to get married now, at a time like this, and so spur-of-the-moment?

Settling down had never been a priority of Michael's, even though he was often spurred on to marry and start a family by well-meaning friends and family who thought a happy home life would complement his thriving career.

"We used to ask Michael, 'When are you going to get married? When are you going to have your firstborn?'" recalls Vicki Palmer, who was an especially close friend of Julius and Jeanne's. According to her, Michael always took the prodding in stride and lightheartedly. "He said, 'I'm going to have a son and name him Cash because I'm going to teach him from the very beginning that it's all about the cash.' That was Michael; he was all about the business."

Kolber arrived in Douglasville to find Michael dressed in a nice suit and ready to go. His once-lumbering frame had shrunken considerably and seemed to be swallowed by the clothing. Kolber could not help but notice how "out of it" his old friend appeared, attributing it to medication. Dena was dressed in a fancy frock and, in Kolber's estimation, looked beautiful though not exactly bridal.

Around two o'clock, the bride and groom presented themselves to the probate office at the Douglas County Courthouse. A cheerful, elderly woman greeted them, ushering the wedding party into a small, windowless room with stacks of large, dusty bound books that Dan recognized as deed records. Awaiting the judge, Dan made small talk with Victor as Dena stood nervously by and Michael collapsed into a chair, too tired and medicated to stand.

"Dena came over and said she needed to talk to me in the hallway," Dan says. "She handed me a paper and said, 'Kolber, I need you to get Michael to sign this.' It was a multi-page power of attorney and final directive. I was shocked she would hand this to me moments before the wedding and I told her so, but she was insistent."

Curious, Michael appeared in the hallway to see what his bride and friend were discussing. Dan had flipped open Dena's document to a page with provisions for cremation, knowing that it would get his friend's immediate attention.

"Mike got a little hot with Dena and made it clear he wasn't going to sign it," Dan recalls. "He didn't want to be cremated, he said, and she sensed this was not something to pursue. I just wanted to get out of there."

The judge, Dan said, "bounded in, all jolly." He was surprised that the man did not inquire about Michael's health or state of mind since even a stranger could tell he was clearly not well. In a matter of a few minutes, Michael and Dena became husband and wife.

"They kissed, I kissed Dena congratulations, shook Michael's hand and said I had to run," Dan says. "I left thinking, 'What the hell just happened?'"

The spring of 2012 put Michael's being to every test. His body was depleted, he had just married Dena under what his family considered to be dubious circumstances and with curious timing, and his finances were shot. Then, at the end of March, his adored mother passed away, leaving behind an assemblage of bereaved sons, daughters and grandchildren who had been well aware of her declining state but were still stricken by the reality of having to carry on without the loving presence—the "beacon of light," as Flem Hollis, Jr., put it—that was Virginia Robinson Hollis.

Michael was somber but seemed to have made peace with his mother's departure. Gary Love says that, at Mrs. Hollis' funeral, "Michael stood over the coffin, repeating that she would see him soon."

Elaine, the doting daughter and sister, had always feared that Michael might fall apart upon their mother's passing. She was relieved that he was much more composed than she had imagined. Still, she noticed a change in him afterward.

"I think he just kind of gave up then," she says. "It seems like he stopped fighting."

In fact, in the weeks immediately following Mrs. Hollis' death, Michael's unscheduled trips to the hospital became more frequent, with ambulances ferrying him from Douglasville to Grady Hospital. Dena was almost always there now, riding with him in the ambulance and keeping watch at his bedside in the hospital suite.

"I would visit throughout the day and even late at night and Dena was there," says Dr. Lewis. "She slept there many nights. I'd go in late at night and come in early in the morning and she was there."

Dena's now-constant presence caused problems for Julius and other family members who, in order to visit Michael, often had to go round-and-around with her about who could come when and for how long. Elaine was one of the few who was welcome to make regular visits, often bringing Michael the short ribs he still craved. Sometimes, he requested the same favorite dish from Flem's wife, Dorothy.

"Two things he did not like: pain and not being in control," recalls Love, who spent a week in the hospital with Michael in early June so Dena could have a break. "He would fuss about the pain—never over the top, but it was a debate between him, the nurses and the doctors about how to manage it."

During his stay at Grady, Gary sat in on all of the doctors' visits. That was how Michael wanted it. He made it known that he wanted Gary involved in all of the important decisions rather than leave them to Dena alone. "If there was a life support issue, it had to have my blessing," Gary said. "No pulling the plug without my consent."

Shortly before Michael was discharged, the physicians raised the matter of "extraordinary measures" that could be available in the end days. Gary was surprised that Michael rejected any intervention that would artificially prolong his life.

"For someone who fought so hard, he decided death-with-dignity would be his last stand," Love says, admiringly. With that, he took his old friend home.

"He was an incredible fighter," Dr. Lewis says. "I wouldn't focus so much on the process of dying because he did it with a fair amount of nobility and he was a good patient."

The weekend before he returned to San Francisco, Gary helped Dena plan a gathering at the Douglasville home so that friends could come and say their farewells. Michael had agreed to the get-together but insisted that it be a small affair, in part because of his low energy and in part because he didn't want to put his deteriorating condition on display.

"Once the word got out, there was a host of folks who wanted to come," Love says. "They decided I was the gatekeeper and started calling me. Let's just say I was able to get Michael to accommodate more than he first approved. He was loved and respected by so many; they just wanted to show it."

Not long after he returned to San Francisco, Michael called again. He was in an ambulance on his way back to the hospital.

"This had happened several times," says Love. "The first time it happened, I could not believe he was calling me from the ambulance. He just wanted to make sure I knew where he was."

But this call was different. Dena got on the phone with Gary and told him that Michael had taken a turn for the worse. In a subsequent call from the hospital, she reported that the doctors were giving her husband medications to keep him comfortable. But the end was near.

"Dena puts the phone to his ear and we hear each other's voice for the last time," says Gary. "He thanked me for all of my support and told me what a great friend I had been. I don't believe he was scared, just sad that it was going to end this way. He was never angry, but he found it hard to believe he was going out like this. He had led a reasonably healthy life—no drugs, ever! —though he did admit his weight probably did him in. It was not quite 'why me,' but just wishing he had more time." Gary allowed himself one long, sad, cleansing cry.

Two days before Michael was discharged from Grady for what would be the last time, Julius hurried to the hospital. There would be no stopping him, no negotiating with Dena this time, he vowed. As he approached Michael's suite, he could hear his brother's still-booming voice. "He was saying, 'Where's Julius, where's Julius?' I just lost it for a moment," Julius says.

At bedside, Julius took Michael's hand, surprised by how strong his grip still was. Looking down on his enfeebled brother, he struggled against the ache that was swelling in his chest. The two of them had weathered so much loss. Their wonderful mother, just three months earlier; sister Ruth in 1987; James Bernard in 2011; and in 2004, Jaison—Julius' tenderhearted, twenty-six-year-old son, felled by a sudden and severe asthma attack during a family retreat at the Hilton Head compound.

"Michael looked at me—his eyes were glazed—and he said, 'Bye, Julius.' I said, 'No, no; it won't be goodbye. It's see you later,'" Julius recalls tenderly. "I said, 'Go on and be with Mama. Go and be with Jaison.'" It would be one of the saddest yet sweetest moments the brothers had ever shared. And their last.

Once back home in Douglasville, Dena called Gary to tell him that Michael was comfortable and that the two of them were drinking champagne. "It's just beautiful," she said.

The end came peacefully on June 18 in the Douglasville home. Gary had left an envelope for Dena and Victor containing the names and numbers of everyone to be called when the sadly inevitable occurred. Victor broke the news to Julius, who in turn notified Elaine and other family members. Victor also called Gary, who suddenly found himself thrust into chaos even though twenty-five-hundred miles away.

"Dena broke down and was not much of a help," he said. "She would not talk to anyone in the family and I had to be the go-between. Julius did all of the planning, all of the arrangements. He did a great job for his brother, but it was stressful dealing with Dena and the family."

When the mortuary officials arrived at the home, they found Dena clinging to her deceased husband. It was the last time the family saw her. She vanished without a word, a letter, or a memento left behind.

It was some time later that Michael's family learned that Dena had gotten rid of most of her husband's belongings in a secret estate sale. His fine clothes, the original Remington sculptures, Michael's player piano—the baby grand that he cherished—were all gone.

So, too, was the lion's share of the finder's fee Michael had received for his work in securing funds for Capital City Bank and Trust. The first of two checks had arrived five days before Michael died. It was for $100,000. Michael gave $80,000 of the proceeds to Dena, as he had promised. Even so, she had refused to help with the funeral expenses for her husband, leaving those costs solely to Julius and Jeanne. Over the next three years—until Capital City folded in 2015—Dena periodically called the bank to inquire about the second check.

"I just wanted something to remember Michael by – a photo, a pencil," says Elaine, whose relationship with Dena had been mostly pleasant. "Dena left and didn't say anything. I pray for her soul every day."

Not even Gary Love's sympathetic appeals could persuade Dena to attend Michael's funeral services. "I tried," he says. "I offered to sit in the last row in the back of the church with her, but it was a no-go. That was the last time I saw or spoke to Dena."

Despite his estranged sister-in-law's intransigence, Julius was more determined than ever that his brother's sendoff would be dignified, formal and commemorative—a tribute to a gifted man whose life, except for its ending, had been conducted on its owner's terms.

It was no secret that Michael had a taste for high quality—his clothing, cars, food, art, music, travel and wine choices all reflected it. But, his pursuit of extraordinary business deals was never really about amassing wealth and material things. Rather, the series of daring deal-making was his answer to a calling deep in his bones to challenge himself in taking on the established powers and beating them at their own game. Michael Hollis loved upsetting the norms, outgunning expectations, pushing the limits. He wanted to prove that, with faith, creativity, preparation and courage, the norms of white privilege can be overturned and power, opportunity, and access can be acquired, even by a black boy from a poor corner of a segregated southern town. He modeled for black Americans the kind of life they should aspire to and the kind of rewards they should expect.

"His world was his family and his work," says Jane Smith, who had known him since childhood. "It was not about showcasing. It was business. He wanted to show what a black man can do. This is the brother who had an airline. This is the one."

Although Michael had an untold number of friends and associates who could have spoken to his talents, persona and achievements, Julius was particular about whom he would ask to take part in his brother's home-going service. The result was a lineup of prominent business, education, and civic leaders sharing poignant and eloquent remembrances that captured Michael's spirit, ambition and accomplishments as brother, friend, businessman, and visionary.

From former U.N. Ambassador and Atlanta Mayor Andrew Young:

Try to figure out what else was on his mind. Where else was he trying to take us? Where else do we need to be in this struggle to make free enterprise and democracy work for the least of these, God's children. That's Michael's legacy.

State Representative Pam Stephenson, Michael's cohort on the Grady board:

I got to see that side of him that loved, loved Grady and loved his family. Because of Michael, we all exist in a dream. Because of Michael Hollis, we all know what it means to fly high. And because of Michael Hollis, I know what it means to have not just a mere presence, but the presence of a true man always loyal to his friends.

From Atlanta Mayor Kasim Reed, describing Michael's legacy:

That an African-American man or person of color believes that they can go to the capital markets, raise money and live their own dreams encompasses the life of Michael Hollis.

I know that the journey for Michael was sometimes thankless, sometimes lonely, but I know that in his heart, he knew it was worth it.

From Dr. Curtis Lewis, the friend and physician who coordinated Michael's care at Grady:

Michael began his life as a Grady baby and ended with receiving his care, out of his choice, at Grady. He may not have had a choice of where he was born, but he did have a choice in where he got his care in the final days of his life. He showed his belief and trust in the institution he loved.

From Nancy Boxill, the Fulton County Commissioner who appointed Michael to the board that managed Grady Hospital:

Michael was a really big man. He was large and solid in every way – in ideas, in charm, in gusto, in confidence, in generosity, in grandeur, in humor and in laughter. He was big and solid and large in his opinions, in his accomplishments, in his caring, in his kindness, in his friendship and in his loyalty. Because he always seemed to be doing big things, people always wanted to know, people always asked, "What is Michael doing now?"

Whatever Michael was doing was risky and whatever Michael was doing was a window into the future. Whatever Michael was doing was a description of possibility. And who wouldn't want to see into the future and grab onto a possibility? That's why we were asking, "What's Michael Hollis doing now?"

And from Dan Kolber, Michael's friend, collaborator, and confidante since their law school days at the University of Virginia:

Michael always had a plan. And he had a Plan B. And he had a plan behind the Plan B. Michael never, ever suffered from analysis paralysis. He would study, he would do his homework and, at the right time, he would spring into action.

Michael had his victories but he also had defeats. But he was always in the arena. If you were lucky enough to be chosen by Michael to participate in his endeavors and you had a ticket to be in the arena with Michael....

Temporarily overcome with emotion, Kolber shook his head and wiped his tears.

Two days after Michael's home-going service, the dignified entombment ritual at Resthaven Memorial Gardens in Decatur, and an elegant repast for thousands at the Four Seasons, Jim Clyburn rose from his leather chair in the U.S. House of Representatives and strode to the well of the chamber.

"Mr. Speaker," he began, "I rise today to pay tribute to a natural born leader, an entrepreneur, a trailblazer and a very dear friend.

"Michael R. Hollis departed this life on June 18, 2012, at the tender age of 58, but not before he achieved his goal to 'do something in life that would make a difference.'"

In a speech read into the Congressional Record, Congressman Clyburn recited a litany of Michael's accomplishments from youth to adulthood. He told his colleagues about Michael's leadership of the Atlanta Youth Congress and his work for Maynard Jackson's campaign. He talked about Michael's selection as a delegate to the White House Conference on Youth and the coveted job he had gotten with the Atlanta Braves' public relations department. He recited Michael's accomplishments at Washington High, Dartmouth College and the University of Virginia School of Law. He informed them of Michael's public service as president of the American Bar Association's Law Student Division and as associate counsel to President Carter's Three Mile Island Commission. He recalled Oppenheimer, Hanover Credit, Blue Sky, Nevis Securities and, of course, Air Atlanta. He noted Michael's heartfelt service to Grady.

"Mr. Speaker," said Congressman Clyburn—by then, the number three Democrat in the U.S. House— "I ask you and our colleagues to join me in honoring Michael R. Hollis, a bright light that was dimmed too soon. He was a remarkable example of what one can accomplish if you hold fast to your dreams. In his own words, he couldn't 'pass through this life and pass up on great opportunities.' His many achievements stand as testaments to a life well lived, and will serve as his lasting legacy."

EPILOGUE

On a wall in his home and in every office he ever had, Michael kept a framed copy of a world-famous passage from President Theodore Roosevelt's speech to a distinguished audience at the Sorbonne in Paris in 1910. There is no wonder that Michael favored that one paragraph from "The Man in the Arena." Its sentiment was the organizing principle of his life.

It is not the critic that counts; not the man who points out how the strong man stumbles or where the do-er of deeds could have done things better. No, the credit belongs to the man who is actually in the arena, who strives valiantly, who knows the great enthusiasms and knows the great devotions and spends himself in a worthy cause so that, at best, he knows the triumph of high achievement and, at worst, if he fails, at least he fails doing greatly so that his place will never be with the cold and timid souls who know neither victory nor defeat.

Michael performed on a variety of playing fields – school, law, politics included—but the business world was his true arena. There, repeatedly, he tested his training regimen—study, observation, planning and innovation—and executed them with confidence, odds and naysayers be damned. Certainly, he knew "the triumph of high achievement."

Several of his friends and associates say Michael was ahead of his time – a recurring observation. Not only was his luxury airline for business travelers a first for the world's busiest airport, but Michael was gifted with a vision that allowed him to foresee market demands. As long ago as 1981, he and two prominent Atlanta businessmen won Mayor Maynard Jackson's support of a project that would transform Hartsfield into an all-inclusive destination for air passengers. The hotel complex proposed by Michael in partnership with developers Ewell Pope and A.J. Land, Jr., included restaurants, shops and entertainment facilities adjacent to the terminals.

"It is my decision to recommend that your firm be the developer of the proposed hotel at Atlanta's new Central Passenger Terminal Complex," Jackson wrote in July 1981. "Now, you and the City, via immediate negotiations, must reach agreement on a proposed contract, which I can recommend to [the] City Council."

The hotel project was not green-lighted then. But, in 2015, City of Atlanta officials approved a $600 million "Airport City" project that would include a travel plaza, residences, office space and a "high-end" hotel with shops and restaurants at Hartsfield. Michael and his partners had come up with the idea thirty-four years too soon.

Who can say what might have become of Michael had the arena not been booby-trapped by race-based prejudices and prohibitions? Without

Maynard Jackson's bold minority contracting mandate, Michael's airline plans might never have even gotten a hearing, given the hostilities and jealousies engulfing the business terrain till then.

What if venture capital had been as available to minority entrepreneurs as it was so readily to white businesses? As late as 2008, a study by two London economists found that "the black/white disparity in startup capital is the largest single factor contributing to racial disparities in closure rates, profits, employment and sales."

What if Equitable and other investors had matched KLM Airlines' $10 million offer and not pulled the plug on Air Atlanta? Equitable had continually contributed huge sums to keep Eastern Airlines flying despite the airline's incurable money woes.

What if the very first doctor Michael consulted when he became ill had pulled out all the stops and ordered the full complement of diagnostic tests and, perhaps discovered the cancer in Michael's pancreas six months earlier? Research by the American Cancer Society and other medical institutions has exposed a "healthcare gap" between whites and people of color related not only to accessibility, affordability and attitudes, but also to a tendency among healthcare professionals to provide less intensive diagnostic and remedial care to non-white patients, irrespective of the patient's means.

The answer to each haunting question is lost to the ages. But, it is easily conceivable that, having accomplished so much from a disadvantaged perch, Michael would only have flown higher and longer had the arena's playing field been level.

And yet, it can be said that Michael Robinson Hollis lived his life fully and memorably. As with Roosevelt's protagonist, he was never among "the cold and timid souls who know neither victory nor defeat."

Shortly after Michael's passing, the Fulton-DeKalb Hospital Authority established The Michael R. Hollis Internship for postsecondary students interested in a range of disciplines, including public health, public policy, public relations, finance, and sociology. The FDHA said the program honors Michael's "legacy of innovation, public service and commitment to health care for all persons, particularly the indigent."

In May 2016, the Atlanta Board of Education voted unanimously to name a new school after Michael. The Michael R. Hollis Innovation Academy offers a Science, Technology, Engineering and Mathematics (STEM) curricula, emphasizing critical thinking, communication skills, project management and teamwork. It adopted "the Six Habits of Hollis" as its canon: collaboration, empathy, communication, self-discipline, creativity, and perseverance.

The new PreK-8 school, in northwest Atlanta, was dedicated in October 2016.

There is no such thing as impossible because it is spelled "I'm possible."

—Unknown author